55 Ways to Have Fun With Google

A cabinet of search engine curiosities, riddles, games, and a little bit of usefulness

Philipp Lenssen

On a spring day you can find your way
to a little flower garden where the Googleheads play
You know they're there by the clothes they wear
And their Googlehead faces and their Googlehead hair.

'Cause they're the Googleheads
They shake their doodleheads
They're the goo-ga-goo-ga-goo-gah Googleheads.
– Laurie Berkner

Contents

Introduction 8

1. Egogoogling: Susan Is… 9

2. The Google Snake Game 15

3. Memecodes: Survival of the Fittest Web Pages 16

4. The Google Irritation Game, and the Google Image Quiz 19

5. Googling Proverbs 20

6. Browsing Images of a Site 24

7. A Brief History of Googlesport 25

8. What is Google, and what do people consider fun about it? 32

9. How Much Time Google Saves Us 37

10. Google Cookin' a Lemon Chicken 40

11. Douglas Adams and the Google Calculator 41

12. Oops, I Googled Again 42

13. The Disappearing Google Logo, a Magic Trick 45

14. Fun With Google Maps, the Wiki Way 46

15. Dave Gorman's Googlewhack 51

16. Google Q&A 54

17. Celebrate Google Non-Weddings, and More 56

18. Design Your SketchUp Dream House 58

19. Kevin Bacon and the Google Network 59

20. The Google Alphabet 62

21. Google Search Tips 63

22. Googlepark 66

23. Googleshare 76

24. The Shortest Google Search (and the One Returning the Most Results) 79

25. Google Rotated and Mini Google 80

26. The Google Quiz: How Much Do You Know About Google? .82

27. Recreate Google From Memory 86

28. The Strange World of Google News 91

29. Aliens Attack Google! 100

30. Top Ten Signs You Are Addicted to Google 102

31. Dig a Hole Through Earth 103

32. Googlebombing 105

33. Google Ads Gone Wrong 109

34. Life in the Age of Google 114

35. Google Hacking..118

36. Googlepolls: Ask the Crowd 121

37. Googlefights...131

38. What If Google Was Evil? Plus: Five Inventions of the Google Future.. 133

39. The Google Adventure Game 150

40. Egobot, Voice of the Web..151

41. Fun Google Gadgets 154

42. Forty-Two, or: A Science-Fiction Interlude 160

43. The Google Book of World Records.. 175

44. Spelling Errors Galore 180

45. Google Groups, Time Machine.. 182

46. Growing a Google Word.. 188

47. Most Popular Words, and PopSents.. 190

48. Create Google Poetry, Prose, and Collages 195

49. Funny Google Videos 203

50. The Realplayer Fish, or: Telling a Story in Synonyms 207

51. Google Parodies... 210

52. The Google Images Prediction Trick...................................... 217

53. Fun With Google Translations 218

54. The Giant Google Painting.. 219

55. Googledromes... 224

Acknowledgments.. 225

Glossary 226

Introduction

This book, in a way, is born out of my daily weblog "Google Blogoscoped" (blog.outer-court.com) and those who read it. Since 2003 I've been writing there covering all things Google – not just the fun stuff, but news, discussion, interviews, tutorials, and everything beyond with a relation to search engines. Thanks to those reading along and providing pointers or feedback, I've been able to discover more interesting pages and get to know more interesting people around the world than ever before.

When I think of Google, first and foremost I think of its role to discover knowledge, people, and people's thoughts. Search engines are truly one of the first emergents of a global brain, and in good tradition of Gutenberg's inventions in the technology of printing, of the invention of the internet, and later the invention of the World Wide Web. All those bring us closer together by speeding up the rhythm in which we communicate.

So there we have it, for the first time in history: search, the key to instant knowledge. And what do we do with it? *Silly things*. OK, not exclusively. But silliness is a part of it. People googlewhack, googlebomb, or egogoogle. People create parodies of Google. They create search engine contests. Magic tricks, riddles and art based on Google. They have a lot of fun with Google, and get together to play games on top of Google services. Even Google Inc themselves send out April Fool's jokes every year, and celebration logos many times a year. Oh, humanity!

But behind many of the playful creations surrounding that giant Google toy, there are serious lessons to be learned. Of the 55 ways to have fun with Google presented here, some ways indeed teach us something; about life, Google, and how to become a better searcher. And the rest of the ways? Well, seriously, they're really just there to have fun. And I hope you enjoy!

1. Egogoogling: Susan Is…

Have you ever searched for your own name on Google, curious what the world has to say about you? Almost everyone of us did, one time or another. In fact, you should – maybe others search for you all the same, and you want to know what they will find.

The act of searching for yourself is also known as "egogoogling." Here's a variant of it which can be a fun game. Enter your first name followed by the word "is" into Google, and put the search in quotes. For example, if your name is Susan, the search would look like this:

"susan is"

Now in the search result snippets, you will learn a lot of things about you that you didn't even know! For the name "Susan," we get the following:

Susan is an amazing person to work with!

Susan is an ethical woman and is refusing to cooperate

Susan is a very attractive young lady (with a boyfriend) who for some reason is always late.

Susan is a top Florida residential real estate agent.

Susan is a top producer specializing in the ski resort town of Breckenridge, as well as the surrounding area.

Not only can you apply this approach to find out more about yourself (or just have a good laugh, actually, as the results are likely to be about *another* person), you can also use this to find out about celebrities. To do so, enter the full celebrity name followed by the word "is" into Google, and put it in quotes again:

"arnold schwarzenegger is"

For action movie star Arnie, we get these results:

Arnold Schwarzenegger is a very talented man who would make an excellent governor.
Arnold Schwarzenegger is falling into a similar spiral.
Arnold Schwarzenegger is looking out for voters' best interests.

> **Arnold Schwarzenegger** is a man more familiar with the red carpets of a movie premiere than a white collar business seminar.
> **Arnold Schwarzenegger** is terrifying as the "killer cyborg" who "looks like Death rendered in steel."
> **Arnold Schwarzenegger is** The Terminator (T-800).
> **Arnold Schwarzenegger is** quickly discovering that life in politics doesn't always produce the happy endings so common in many of his Hollywood blockbusters.

Note that you can use "stars in," "was born in" and similar glue words instead of "is" to find out almost anything about a celebrity. You can even expand the idea to include things, not people... try searching for "Nikon cameras are" and similar queries.

If you don't have Google near you, here are some popular male and female names with their "egogoogled" results.

Male Names

Aaron is a monotonic anchor.
Adam is a deeply disturbing and depressing film.
Alan is AI's pattern-matching chatbot.
Albert is so cute!
Andrew is the Patron Saint of Scotland.
Anthony is probably the best male vocal out there.
Arthur is kind of in a category by itself.
Brandon is for the birds.
Brian is embarrassed that he needs the extra help in school.
Carl is just sitting there in Nashville!
Charles is also a coach of AYSO youth soccer, an officer in the PTA of the local elementary school.
Christopher is of mixed heritage (Asian-American).
Daniel is a natural talent .
David is not allowed computer access.
Dennis is one of Britain's best known entrepreneurs.
Donald is rarely easy to understand, and people have supposedly heard him say all sorts of risque things. Donald is a Professor in the Department of Psychology.
Douglas is "King of California."
Edward is a biological human (not a robot).
Edward is coming BACK to television.
Eric is featured on guitar and mandolin on the songs Viargra and Gypsy woman.
Frank is hilariously funny on what makes us red-staters different from blue-staters (not).
Fred is leading the Franklin Templeton Shootout after 2 rounds!

Gary is the editor and compiler of ResourceShelf.
George is, quite simply, the worst helpdesk technician ever.
Gerald is frightened and doesn't understand why the woman wants to assist him.
Gregory is recognized as one of the very foremost orators.
Harold is an original.
Henry is currently in jail.
Jack is looking for a house with about half an acre of land to buy in California.
James is as forthright as an Old Testament prophet.
Jason is who the JASON Project is named after.
Jeffrey is helping to clear up this cosmic murkiness.
Jeremy is a conscientious worker who can usually be relied upon.
Jerry is a master at understanding your goals for the photograph and then creating the perfect lighting.
Joe is "LIVE" daily.
John is succeeding marvelously in journalism's highest calling: to encourage people .
Jonathan is writing a magical fable of his grandfather's village in Ukraine.
Joseph is the Special Assistant to the President and Senior Director.
Joshua is home now.
Juan is similar to the one at the top of this page.
Justin is practicing walking on his hands.
Keith is a true character who comes across as being very sincere.
Kenneth is a strong advocate for community building and social change.
Kevin is creative director and co-founder at Lightroom.
Larry is also a political planner.
Lawrence is a New York Real Estate Broker specializing in Putnam.
Mark is coauthor of Inside Windows 2000, Third Edition (Microsoft Press).
Matthew is believed to have used Mark and the theoretical source.
Michael is abandoning the music business to release his songs online for free instead.
Patrick is one of the nation's best young auto racers.
Paul is backwards in line and taller than everyone else, again.
Peter is a consultant with a distinguished academic track record.
Ralph is not beyond fishing around for a philosophical explanation.
Raymond is an observer-participant anthropologist in the Internet
Richard is often accused of being overly concerned with himself.
Robert is an elder in the Presbyterian Church (USA)
Roger is approached by a gangling, spotty computer scientist.
Ronald is known in more than 100 countries wherever you find McDonald's restaurants.
Ryan is clearly good at her job.
Samuel is irresistible.
Scott is arguably the most well-known and influential unknown composer.
Shawn is now 26 years old, lives in San Diego, enjoys snowboarding, taking trips to Lake.
Stephen is working with Marvel to produce a series of comic books.
Steve is a DJ in Boston.

Steven is writing the same song over and over.

Terry is back with his new group, The Society for Truth and Justice.

Thomas is still searching

Timothy is an accomplished juggler.

Walter is now 79 years of age and in excellent health.

William is truly "fit for a king."

Female Names

Alice is an AIML engine written in C++.

Amanda is most known for her role in FOX's hit TV show "The OC."

Amy is... sniff... sniff... sad about our recent barking on her "Re-name RSS contest."

Angela is absolutely swamped this week!

Ann is only a writer – and NOT a private detective.

Anna is helping out with the hurricane relief effort.

Anne is a storyteller.

Barbara is to go to Paddle Sports of Santa Barbara.

Betty is distinctively heard singing alongside Michael.

Brenda is the mother of 14 children, 12 of whom are adopted.

Carolyn is currently training for the next WNBA season.

Catherine is a star.

Christina is also busy promoting the line of footwear "Skechers."

Christine is red and white.

Cindy is in "love with the attention."

Cynthia is still on the border.

Debbie is an International Magician.

Deborah is pleased to announce two brand-new paintings!

Debra is a nationally recognized expert on communication skills.

Denise is funny, bright and bubbly.

Diana is currently in London, England where she is working on the artwork.
...

Diane is steadfast in her mission of marketing and negotiating the terms of the sale.

Donna is recording her 2nd CD, "Feels Like Home", which will be released in 2001.

Doris is such a great zine.

Dorothy is 5 Dinosaur years old, and is very wise for her age.

Edith is only meaningful.

Elizabeth is just south of the expanding Addo Elephant National Park.

Ellen is Africa's first lady president.

Emily is nation's young poet of the year.

Heather is the one with the muscles.

Helen is Coming To Town!.

Irene: Irene is a wedding and portrait photographer serving parts of New England and New York State. Jane is one of Victorian literature's rebellious heroines.

Janet is fantastic.

Janice is right there on that edge.

Jennifer is a genius.

Jessica is a joy and a delight that brings happiness to all of us.

Josephine is Under Construction!

Judith is no mythical personage.

Judy is going to still have to answer to a higher authority.

Julie is no longer a loner; she, too, learns about being a part of a community.

Karen is an experienced tutor in both fiddle and step dance.

Katherine is one of two large towns you will come across on the route between Darwin and Alice.

Kathleen is foremost a musician.

Kathy is married to Rick Hilton, who is the wealthy grandson.

Kimberly is married to Johnny.

Laura is not a psychologist nor a psychiatrist.

Linda is now going to move to the south of Sweden.

Lisa is furious with Debbie.

Louise is a first-class song, there is no doubting.

Margaret is not the enemy.

Marie is an accomplished author with an important story to tell.

Martha is "free."

Melissa is very open about her past.

Michelle is as Michelle does.

Nancy is also an award-winning video producer.

Nicole is now working hard on a NEW collection of tunes.

Pamela is coming into her glory today.

Rachel is well on her way to achieving her goals.

Rebecca is never seen, and yet she is the main character.

Ruth is a member of the American Immigration Lawyers Association.

Sandra is the fourth woman to win it all, compared to only three men.

Sara is right. Yes, it is true.

Sarah is still in the studio working.

Sharon is expected to decide this weekend.

Sherry is a type of wine originally produced in and around the town of Jerez.

Stephanie is so afraid of germs, she can't stop washing her hands.

Susan is creative, perceptive, intuitive, and timely.

Suzanne is not Sue.

Tina is no acronym.

Virginia is a five-day bike tour.

Wendy is now the only comic featured on the website.

(Original cartoon by the US government.)

2. The Google Snake Game

Here's a party game which needs nothing but a working internet connection (say, a notebook or cell phone), and Google.com's web search. The goal is to create the longest phrase that Google can find by alternately adding one word to the end of the other player's search phrase. Say, the first person starts with "Feelings". Now the second person adds a word, "are", so we get "Feelings are"... (Note the use of quotation marks in the search query.)

Now every time a word is added, the phrase is searched for in Google, and the resulting page count is announced to the group. The one person who creates a sentence with zero results in Google loses and has to do something silly (or if you want to play with points, he loses a point, and the last person who created a sentence with results in Google will win a point). To prevent cheating, the one whose turn is next is not allowed to look at any search result snippet.

Let's take our sample, and see what we get:

Peter: "Feelings" (53,200,000 results in Google)
Mary: "Feelings are" (2,100,000 results)
Jake: "Feelings are nothing" (1,090 results)
Susan: "Feelings are nothing and" (19 results)
Peter: "Feelings are nothing and we" (0 results)

Susan gets 1 point, and Peter gets minus 1 points (or has to do something silly).

If you create too obscure a sentence there won't be any results and you will lose, but if your sentence gets too many results, your opponent will also be able to create a sentence with results. The basic strategy is to try to create sentences so silly that there are only a few results, but not so silly there are no results...

3. Memecodes: Survival of the Fittest Web Pages

Memecodes are web pages with randomly created texts which are born and die over the course of time. How is that possible? By basing those pages on the rules of evolution: the more often a page is found and clicked on in Google – the more popular it is – the more offspring it produces.

The title *Memecodes* is a word play on Richard Dawkins *memes* from his book "The Selfish Gene"[1]. In it, he wrote:

> Examples of memes are tunes, ideas, catch-phrases, clothes fashions, ways of making pots or of building arches. Just as genes propagate themselves in the gene pool by leaping from body to body via sperms or eggs, so memes propagate themselves in the meme pool by leaping from brain to brain via a process which, in the broad sense, can be called imitation.

I created this experiment in early 2004 to watch it grow, with some interesting results. Here's how it worked in detail. First, based upon a dictionary of words, pages with random texts were created. To make sure the texts looked rather natural, words like "the" or "and" as well as punctuation were added. The resulting pages contained Jabberwockyish[2] paragraphs such as this one:

> Cognac? Is sloth is waist is declare of bramble flood in of stoical. Footman... Hesitancy a for attention flabby wanton and calculate vtol cyclamate that paprika feign the aline fourth qualifications of in. Thatch, Saccharin hansom rationale in dine numbers.

This page – or set of "genes" – was unique in the whole set of pages which made up the "ecosystem." Now there was a possibility certain sentences or fragments of sentences made sense. One sentence, for example, contained the phrase "corpulent pigeons," which someone did indeed search for in Google. As soon as that happened and the searcher clicked on the Memecodes result, this particular page created offspring – it "mated" with the searcher, if you will. The offspring of any page was the same page slightly mutated by randomly replacing some of its words. This way, maybe "corpulent pigeons" became "corpulent pink pigeons" (surely that would have had the chance to be an even more successful gene) or it could turn into "corpulent tower pigeons" (and face certain death over time, because rarely do people search for such a thing!).

How did pages die then? There was a page population limit of a little over 2,000 pages. Whenever a new page was born, the oldest page would be removed (the link from the front-page of the Memecodes experiment pointing to this page would be removed). If a page didn't manage to create offspring until then, its genes were unsuccessful in surviving and would therefore not be continued.

Other genes (random texts) would be more successful, though. And some of the successful pages would become even more successful in turn, possibly finding a natural search niche to settle into: they lured more and more searchers to find them by creating more and more "natural language." One day, the pages might even turn into Shakespeare, and it wouldn't need infinite monkeys to pull it off! Or rather, that was my hope. But evolution takes a lot of time to show results, and after little more than a year, I stopped the experiment. Until then, however, a lot of people found their way onto the site and thus produced offspring. All in all, a walloping 10,022 pages were born (about 2,500 of those seed pages created automatically in the beginning), with some Memecodes in their 5th generation.

Some of the popular sentences were truly strange, like "feel the wrath of salivating mushroom eating frog aliens with microwave ovens," or the more down-to-earth "seagull sandwich." Other sentences were circling around the word "torrent," because "Torrents" had started to become a popular way to download video and other files on the web. The only clearly recognizable pattern in successful genes, however, were exotic words and word combinations I can't even print here for reasons you might be able to guess: they were all about "adult" topics. Then again, I guess that's nature!

End Notes

1. Dawkins, R. (1976). *The Selfish Gene.* (www.55fun.com/3.1)

2. *Jabberwocky* is the title of a nonsensical poem from Lewis Carroll's *Through the Looking-Glass and What Alice Found There* (1872). It starts off with "Twas brillig, and the slithy toves/ Did gyre and gimble in the wabe." (www.55fun.com/3.2)

4. The Google Irritation Game, and the Google Image Quiz

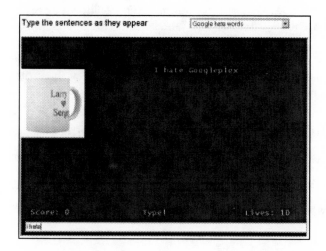

This is probably the weirdest game on Google you will find online. **"Bemmu's Cure for Google Irritation"** (www.55fun.com/9.1) moves all kinds of Google-related sentences through the screen. Like "I hate Googleplex," "Who needs Larry," or "Google doesn't frighten me." Now it's your job to type these sentences into a small box below the screen as fast as you can before they disappear. When you succeed, you get as many points as the phrase contains letters. If you don't succeed, you lose one of your 10 lives.

If you are looking for a little more long-term fun, I suggest my **Google Image Quiz** (blog.outer-court.com/quiz/). In it, you will be presented with 15 images for every round. Then it's your job to find the correct search words that were used to find these images in Google Images. Sounds easy? Give it a try, I've heard it's addicting, too!

5. Googling Proverbs

In his book *Was Wir Wissen¹* ("what we know"), German author Benjamin von Stuckrad-Barre tried to find the everyday life contexts in which proverbs are used – and he used Google to do so. For example, he searched for "Those who live in glass houses should not throw stones" and then listed *who* was being referred to on the resulting web pages (like discussion boards, or news articles). Let's follow the same approach for English proverbs here!

Who shouldn't throw stones in a glass house?

- The plywood industries of Malaysia and Indonesia
- People who say Michael is guilty
- Those who tell on people who don't follow a site's Terms of Service
- Russia
- People who call Greeks liars

What conquers all?

- Love
- Labor and perseverance
- Courage
- Truth
- Humor
- Linux

What can't a man live by alone?

- Bread
- Rice
- Incompetence
- Crimefighting
- Chocolate

- Bagels
- Jaffa Cakes

What's not everything?

- Money
- Winning the prize, or the tournament
- Wikipedia
- Salad
- Ecology
- Speed
- Base salary
- Technological superiority

What best things in life are free?

- Sun Java Studio Enterprise 8.0
- Computers
- The Chicago Cultural Center's top-notch music programming
- Online Black Jack
- Business opportunities
- A smile
- Seattle

Who let the dogs out?

- 49ers
- Karl, Bob, and Paulie
- Rumsfeld
- FOX
- Karl Rove
- Nintendo

What is the new black?

- Lurid pink
- Keylogging
- Green Teat
- Fluffy
- Gray, or fuchsia, or red
- Caucasian
- UNPOP
- Benjamin
- Simplicity
- BeOSmodule
- Scrolling
- Blacker
- Polygamy
- Apathy
- Pacifism
- Downshifting

What shouldn't you throw out with the bathwater?

- Musicians
- The crown
- The pervert
- The BabyCenter.com
- The leak
- The monitor
- The culture
- The dressed up chihuahua
- The concept of rural
- The artistic effort
- The Furbies
- The appraisal

- God
- SOAP
- Pearls
- The fluoride

End Notes

1. Stuckrad-Barre, B.v. (2005). *Was Wir Wissen.* (www.55fun.com/5)

6. Browsing Images of a Site

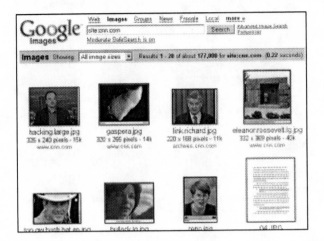

If you want to see all images of a particular website, you can use the "site:" operator on Google Images (images.google.com) – you may know this operator from Google's web search. For example, enter *site:cnn.com* into the Google Images search box to see all images shown on CNN's website. Click on an image in the result list and you're taken to the respective page containing the image.

This approach is fun if you want to visually explore a site, and you are not interested in any particular content on that site. However, you can still combine the site search with an additional keyword. A search for *site:cnn.com clinton* would therefore show CNN's images of President Bill Clinton, or images related to him.

Want to try this out on a site a little more fun than CNN? I suggest you enter the following for thousands of riveting photo illusions: *site:worth1000.com*

7. A Brief History of Googlesport

It may be that all games are silly. But then, so are humans.
– Robert Lynd

People today often participate in a challenge called "Search Engine Optimization contests." In a nut-shell, the goal of these contests is to get to be the top ranked page in the Google search results for a given term or phrase. In order to not disturb "normal" search results, contests often take nonsensical words as their target. While in the beginning I was often taking part in these contests myself, after many lessons learned (including a contest for the nonsense phrase "Seraphim Proudleduck") today I do not participate in them anymore. But before we jump into the history of search engine *optimization* contests, let's go back several thousand years and start recapping the history of search engines themselves.

B.C-1956: The Dawn of Computing

Before Christ, there was the counting aid Abacus. Some centuries later, in 1642, Blaise Pascal builds a mechanical calculator. Around 1820, Charles Babbage follows-up with his steam-powered Difference Engine, and Countess of Lovelace Augusta Ada Byron is pondering programming it after having met him.

The first computer (a programmable calculator) by German engineer Konrad Zuse is completed in 1941.

Britain and USA take over the computing technology field with Colossus, ENIAC, the transistor (by Bell Telephone), and UNIVAC – the "Universal Automatic Computer."

1957-1990: The Internet

In 1957, ARPA (the Advanced Research Projects Agency, within the Department of Defense, DoD) is created to foster US technology. Some ten years later, DARPA marks the beginnings of the Internet. Intel is founded in '68, Doug Engelbart spends time show-casing his revolutionary ideas of word processing, and a year later, Xerox creates the equally revolutionary think tank PARC, the Palo Alto Research Center. Universities are slowly being connected together via ARPANET in 1969. In 1977, Apple II is born, followed by the IBM

PC in '81. 1984, the year of cyberpunk novel Neuromancer, sees the introduction of the Domain Name System (DNS).

In the late '80s, the number of Internet hosts breaks 100,000, and people are starting to get lost. In 1990, before the days of the World Wide Web, McGill University student Alan Emtage creates FTP indexing search tool Archie. One year later, Mark McCahill introduces the alternative Gopher. Veronica (Archie's girlfriend in the comic books, and the "grandmother of search engines") appears on the scene in 1992, spidering Gopherspace texts, and Jughead arrives in '93.

1990-1993: WWW, and WWWW

In the meantime, the World Wide Web, created by Tim Berners-Lee and released by CERN (the European Organization for Nuclear Research) in '91, is starting to take off. And 1993, the year the first web browser Mosaic takes the world by storm, also sees the first acclaimed web robot, Matthew Gray's World Wide Web Wanderer. Martijn Koster announces meta-tag spidering Aliweb in late '93.

1994: Search Engines See the Light

The World Wide Web is becoming the most important internet service. Pizza can be ordered online, and soon Sun will give birth to Java programming technology. (The Java motto was "write once, run everywhere," but frustrated programmers around the world later changed it to "write once, debug everywhere.")

In early 1994, Jerry Yang and David Filo of Stanford University start Yahoo! in an attempt to exert some kind of order on an otherwise anarchic collection of documents. (The word Yahoo is short for "Yet Another Hierarchical Officious Oracle," but was pretty much looked up randomly in a dictionary by the two Yahoo founders – the two creators say they liked the name because they considered themselves yahoos.)

Some months later in Washington, Brian Pinkerton's WebCrawler is getting about its work; over at Carnegie Melon, Dr. Michael Maldin creates Lycos (the name comes from the Latin wolf spider).

1995-1997: Dot-Com Rising

More and more search engines appear. There's Metacrawler, Excite (in late 1995), AltaVista (late 1995), Inktomi/ HotBot (mid-1996), Ask Jeeves and GoTo. Yahoo, actually a directory, is the leader, but AltaVista – meaning "a view from above," and being a wordplay on (Palo) Alto-Vista – launched in 1995 and brought some fierce competition. In 1997 AltaVista was bought by Compaq and we have some right to assume this and a resulting lost focus brought its downfall.

1998-2002: Google et al

It's late 1998. Stanford's Larry Page and Sergey Brin reinvent search ranking technology with their paper "The Anatomy of a Large-Scale Hypertextual Web Search Engine" and start what some time later becomes the most successful search engine in the world: Google (Larry misspells "Googol," which is a really large number, and Sergey draws the colorful logo on his own using the free GIMP painting software). The uncluttered interface, speed and search result relevancy were cornerstones in winning the tech-savvy people, who were later followed by pretty much everyone looking for something online. Other contenders, like MSN, are left in the dust. In September 1999, Google leaves Beta.

Search engine optimization in the meantime becomes a bigger and bigger business, with experts and amateurs alike trying to boost rankings of websites, more often than not for commercial reasons.

In 2000, Yahoo and Google become partners (Yahoo is using Google's search technology on their own site for a while). In late 2000, Google is handling over 100 million daily search requests.

In 2001, AskJeeves (which dropped the "Jeeves" in the meantime) acquires Teoma, and GoTo is renamed to Overture.

2003-Now: The Dawn of Search Engine Contests

It's hard to tell which search engine contest truly was first. People have been competing to get on top of search results for commercial reasons pretty much since the invention of search engines, and the employed tactics are called "Search Engine Optimization." But so-called "SEO contests" are created mostly to have fun, and to shed more light on Google's ranking secrets – and potential methods for abusing those rankings. At times, there were also prizes up for grabs during the contests. Some of those even got handed over to the winner (not all, mind you – it's a fun sport in a shady environment!).

Today, there are so many different SEO contests going on at any given time it's hard to keep track of them all. I'll list some of the first, some of which I participated in myself with the weblog "Google Blogoscoped."

2004: SERPs

SERPs is short for "Search Engine Result Pages" (completely coincidentally, it also means "State Earnings-Related Pension Scheme"). It was the target keyword for a search engine optimization contest. A group of people, myself included, started the challenge in a search engine discussion group and came up with the term "SERPs" on January 16, 2004. The term was both self-referential, which was fun, and relatively harmless (presumably not a lot of people were searching for it, as there were only 30,700 pages prior to the contest – that may sound much, but it's only about $1/10^{th}$ the page count a search for *pink speaker manuals* yields).

I started my own entry as a normal blog post in "Google Blogoscoped," wanting to see how it would fare in the contest (it was pushed out of the top ten pretty soon). However the leading entry on Google's blogging community Blogspot was deserted by its owner, Sam, and I was able to open up a site with the same name, thus sitting on his top-ranked page now. Sam's tactic (which included leaving a lot of links in website guest-books, an approach rightfully deemed spam) made his page the winner on February 16th, 2004.

Kebapgraz

The "Kebapgraz" SEO competition owes its name to "Döner Kebap," a Turkish dish popular in Germany and Austria, and the Austrian city Graz. Most of the participants of this challenge were from Germany or Austria, using German-language pages. The contest started on June 16, 2004, as a follow-up to a previous challenge for "Haltezeitmessungen." Linkfarms (a large group of interlinked websites trying to increase their Google PageRank) or other kind of spam were not allowed in this contest. The end date was September 10, 2004, and the amount of web pagescontaining the word went from 0 to 167,000 later on. A German wiki entry (a wiki usually is a encyclopedia-style website which everyone can help edit) was inhibiting the top rank for almost all the time, only to be pushed to number two in a 24 hour period starting shortly before the end date.

The contest was started by David Reisner, aged 17, from Austria. "One day I thought, there are some funny contests going on, but there was no Kebap on the web" David said. I asked him for lessons learned, and he answered one should think about the exact competition rules beforehand to avoid some longer fights he's been through. He added: "In SEO there is a nice tip: give and you will be given, be it advice, links or content."

Schnitzelmitkartoffelsalat and Gepardenforellen

Yet another German-language Google contest was the hunt for "Schnitzelmitkartoffelsalat" (which translates to *steak with potato salad*). It was started by Steffi Abel on November 15, 2002, in a German discussion group. At that time the word *Schnitzelmitkartoffelsalat* did not return any pages in Google. More than three years later, 22,000 occurrences can be found. According to German webmaster Lars Kasper, who covered the challenge on his website, variations of the *Schnitzelmitkartoffelsalat* challenge included the nonsense words "Telefondesinfizierstudium" (*the study of phone desinfection*) and "Walnichtfischmitkartoffelsalat" (*whale, not fish, with potato salad*).

Some time later, German Googlesport really took off with the creation of the "Hommingberger Gepardenforelle" contest ("Gepardenforelle" translates to "Homminghill leopard trout"). It was launched by Germany's biggest IT magazines (on- and offline) and the two keywords today return almost 3 million web pages.

Mangeur de Cigogne

And then, there was a French Googlesport contest for the phrase "Mangeur de Cigogne." Launched by Promo-Web, the games began in March 2004, and were to be ended in June 15 2004. This might have been one of the weirdest and most obsessive of all search engine optimization contests. And naturally, because most content was French, you couldn't understand a word of what happened unless you were fluid in this language.

So what does "Mangeur de Cigogne" mean? It literally translates to "eaters of stork." But, according to Jerome Chesnot from the south of

France, "It means nothing really. This string was chosen to not pollute Google results."

Jerome held the 1st place in this competition for the 15 last days, but then came in second. He told me *Mangeur de Cigogne* was "really a good experience ... in terms of HTML optimization and other technical things."

Nigritude Ultramarine

"Nigritude Ultramarine" was arguably the biggest SEO contest that ever took place. It received enormous coverage including articles on Wired.com and tech site Slashdot. The competition was started by SEO company DarkBlue (hence the name "Nigritude Ultramarine," which is another way to say "dark blue").

Blogger Anil Dash nearly won the top rank in the first round ending June 7, 2004 with a blog entry (the second round prize, a 17" LCD flat screen, went to the aggressive contenders of a web discussion forum). Anil's post was linked from various other high-profile blogs who wanted to push a friend up the Google rankings. Anil wanted to prove that good old content – as opposed to sleazy optimization tactics – is king, and he was successful in doing so.

As I'm writing this, there are around 215,000 web pages containing the phrase "Nigritude Ultramarine." Anil Dash is still number one.

A Short Guide to SEO

So how do you win these search engine optimization contests in the first place? This depends on the search engine, but for Google, heavy "on-page" optimization is futile in a competitive environment, and all depends on "off-page" optimization.

To explain, "on-page" optimization means you create a page which repeats the target keywords in a variety of places, in the meta keywords, in the title, in page headings and so on. What you do on your page might have an effect on the human reader – which is indeed important – but it's of little value to the Googlebot and the way Google ranks your site. For competitive keywords, all that Google is interested in is this: *how many important pages link to your page using the target keywords as link text?*

If you can get a lot of valuable "backlinks" from authoritative web pages (say, a mainstream news site, or a #1 blog for an industry), then a high ranking will come naturally. So, the real key is to get good backlinks (ideally links containing the target keywords). Not necessarily 1000s of them; it's of more value to get a dozen high-value backlinks, then a million low-value backlinks. For example, Google pretty much ignores it when you create 100,000 backlinks from your website A which point to your website B (and creating such a huge amount of links is not too hard with the help of server-side programming). Google understands that such "close-knit" networks aren't showing natural authority – they might easily be faked by so-called spam farms… and spamming is one thing Google in their rankings try to avoid.

Now how do you get all those links from others? Here, we need to forget about technical optimization for a second. What's important now is to have great web page content, and to make it be known to the right people – not by mass-mailing everyone and their dog, but by submitting your link to blogs on the subject, emailing the right people, pitching your story to mainstream news sites, or sharing it in newsgroups or web forums relevant to your site. Outside of an SEO competition, that means you need to understand a community, be part of it, and help others. People won't link to boring and perhaps over-optimized pages, but people will link to pages that help them (or make them laugh). They link to a tutorial, a good read, a funny video, a cartoon, or an interesting photo. Within the scope of an SEO competition, it's also likely that people simply link to a friend. If you're actively participating in making the web a better place for all (content is king!), you'll also be getting your share of "link love."

8. What is Google, and what do people consider fun about it?

Miki, don't move. Everything is going to be OK.
There is just nowhere to hide from Google any more.

(Image courtesy of Elwyn Jenkins. © 2003 Verity Intellectual Properties Pty Ltd.)

Google is more than just the search engine. Even though that alone wouldn't be too bad, either, because it allows us to quickly receive answers from the web to almost any question asked. Today while I'm writing this book, Google consists of dozens of services (google.com/sitemap.html). Some you may have heard of, like Gmail, or Google Maps. Others are more obscure, like Google Base, Google Page Creator, Google Writely or Google X, and even Google experts can have a hard time keeping track.

To understand what people know of Google – and what they think is fun about it – I asked my sister Judith about the different services. Afterwards, I asked UK programmer and Google expert Tony Ruscoe (ruscoe.net/blog/) about these services. Both were urged to take a guess in case they were clueless about the answer. Well, who's right then? I won't judge, but instead will let you read their answers now!

Asking a Google Novice

Judith, what is Google Talk?

Judith: I believe that's a text to speech program to read out things for you.

What is Google Earth?

Judith: I know that one! You can view the whole globe from above. You can zoom close into every country.

What is Picasa?

Judith: That's a fun drawing program to create Picasso-like paintings.

What is Gmail?

Judith: That's an email client.

What are the Google Labs?

Judith: That's a place to propose interesting ideas for Google to add to their products. The suggestions are filtered by Google engineers and finally, they will be implemented.

What is Google Maps?

Judith: I don't have a clue.

What is Google Scholar?

Judith: Google for students, without any adult websites.

What is Google Video?

Judith: That's a search engine, similar to an image search, but for videos instead.

What is Google Images?

Judith: The same like a search engine for words, but with images.

What is Google Answers?

Judith: That's a place where you can ask questions for other people to answer. If the answer is right, those who answered will get money.

What is Google Catalogs?

Judith: You can see pages taken from catalogs, for example when you enter "teddy bear," you will see catalog pages containing teddy bears.

What is Froogle?

Judith: That could be a parody site acting just like Google... no matter what you enter, all you get are results containing images of frogs.

What are Google Alerts?

Judith: That's when Google sees you are searching for illegal material online and you click on one of the result pages. This can have legal consequences.

What is Google Blogger?

Judith: That's a weblog community run by Google.

What is Google Desktop?

Judith: That's like Microsoft Windows but made by Google. E.g. it contains a word processor.

What are Google Groups?

Judith: Those are chat rooms on any conceivable topic. You can login to talk.

What is Google X?

Judith: I have no idea! Well, I suppose it's a kind of Google-related riddle or puzzle game.

What do you think is fun about Google?

Judith: Searching for people. That's nothing particularly special or uncommon, but it satisfies your curiosity about someone you want to know more about.

Asking a Google Expert

Tony, what is Picasa?

Tony: It's a photo management/ organization application. You can download a program that allows you to manipulate your images.

What is Google Talk?

Tony: It's an IM – Instant Messenger – application that allows online conversations and VoIP, Voice over IP.

What is Google Earth?

Tony: It's fantastic! I've told my friends that it's arguably the best thing to appear on the Internet this year! Seriously though, it's a program that allows you view the earth from space. You can zoom in and view certain areas really close up.

What is Google Labs?

Tony: In my view, Google Labs isn't really a service as such. It's simply a name they give to many new releases that don't quite make it to Beta. It often consists of smaller projects that some of the Google Employees create in their 20% time.

What is Google Local?

Tony: It's pretty much like an online service directory, like the Yellow Pages. In fact, Google Local UK uses Yell.com for its results, I think. It's recently been integrated with Google Maps so that it's easier to see where the businesses are located.

What is Google Scholar?

Tony: It's an online search that searches educational papers and theses, things like that.

What is Google Video?

Tony: It's a video search that searches for videos that have been uploaded by the public or by a number of different associations who have agreed to let their content be available for free. I think it only searches the description or transcript that's been provided by the user.

What is Google Answers?

Tony: Google Answers is an "ask the expert" service where you can submit a question, name your price and, hopefully, get an answer from an expert in the field.

What is Froogle?

Tony: It's an online price comparison service to help you with your online shopping.

What are Google Alerts?

Tony: Basically, Google will send you an email whenever something new appears in the Google web results or Google News.

What is Google Desktop?

Tony: Google Desktop started off as a desktop application – Google Desktop Search – that enabled you to search your PC for information. I think it's turned into something much bigger now, where you can add your own bits to it. I've never used it.

What are Google Groups?

Tony: Google Groups encapsulates Usenet groups as well as Usenet-style groups that have been created by Google Account owners. They are basically discussion forums/ mailing-lists.

What was Google X?

Tony: I think it was a service similar to the existing home page that used a Mac OS X style interface. It appeared in Google Labs but then disappeared. Presumably because of legal reasons... but we don't know. I never saw it, but I've seen some copies of it.

What is Google Base?

Tony: Good question. It seems to be everything! It's an online suppository where people can upload practically any data that has a structure. It can be used for storing things like recipes, people profiles and classified ads. So you can advertise anything you might have for sale – although there's no way to take payment via Google Base at the moment. In short, it's an online database application.

What is Google Analytics?

Tony: It's a web stats analysis application. You place some JavaScript in your website which then collects data from your visitors using cookies. Google Analytics takes all this data and analyzes it, creating graphs and reports about your visitors' trends.

What is Google Sets?

Tony: It's in Google Labs. I looked at it a long time ago so I've forgotten exactly what it does! I think it's a service that lets you provide several items – up to five, I think – and Google will suggest some more items that are in the same group.

What do you think is fun about Google?

There are a lot of things that make Google fun. It can be used to settle the most basic of arguments. We often use it in the office when we don't believe what someone is saying. We run the risk of being fooled by the "If it appears on Google, it's true!" rule!

Their services are always interesting. Waiting for a new service can be exciting. It gets people talking...

Very often, the services aren't ground-breaking – but the way Google present them is. Take Gmail and Google Maps. These types of services had been around for years, yet all of a sudden you could just sit and play with Google Maps for hours!

9. How Much Time Google Saves Us

We might forget how much fun a search engine is, and how much time it saves us in doing everyday things, until the internet connection is interrupted and we're left without Google. (Or, and this happens more rarely, when Google itself is down.) But usually after some minutes, things are back to normal – and we got our extended memory, our library of more books we could ever read, our information center, and our universal answer machine. And now, for just a moment, I would like you to imagine what today's life would be *without* all that. What life would be without Google... and how much more time we'd be spending on solving our problems.

Finding Your Lost Keys

With Google: You enter "How to find lost keys" into Google, and the pages you find suggest to search every place again. *Time spent: 10 minutes.*

Without Google: You search your rooms. You start to get angry, then desperate. You search for a second time, and find your keys. *Time spent: 10 minutes.*

Time saved using Google: none.

Opening a Coconut

With Google: You search for "How to open a coconut." A video tutorial explains you should hold a coconut over a bowl, and use the blunt side of a cleaver to whack the coconut until it cracks open in two halves. *Time spent: 5 minutes.*

Without Google: You ask your neighbor, and she tells you she doesn't know either, but invites you to check her cookbooks collection. On that day, you fall in love with her, and she with you. You discover the solution to the coconut problem in her books the next morning. *Time spent: 1 day.*

Time saved using Google: around 1 day, but love life suffers.

Checking If Tonight's Date Is Trustworthy

With Google: You enter "Frank Simmonz" into Google. His criminal records turn up, and you stay away from him. *Time spent: 5 minutes.*

Without Google: You meet Frank Simmonz. He seems to be a nice guy, not poor either, and he's elegantly dressed. You meet him again at a restaurant a week later. Another week after that, you notice Frank has blood on his shirt but you try to not mention it. Later, while you two watch a mafia movie together, Frank says, "People in that business talk differently, and I should know!" You leave the cinema in a hurry. *Time spent: 2 weeks.*

Time saved using Google: 1 week, 6 days, 23 hours, and 55 minutes.

Creating a Revolutionary Method of Transportation

With Google: You enter "how to speed up transportation" into Google and stumble upon a tutorial on wheels construction. *Time spent: 1 minute.*

Without Google: You go out and watch nature. You also analyze people, and animals, trying to figure out how and why they move. You make sketches, you observe, and you remain patient. You dabble with rocks, wood, and water. You teach your children about what you learned during your lifetime, sparking their curiosity. After that, your children take over the task you began and try finding a revolutionary method of transportation. And their children, too. The idea spreads to neighbors, friends and family, and it spans generations.

Then, a whole culture becomes infested with the problem, and everyone everywhere is trying to crack their head solving it. Many, many years later, the wheel is invented. *Time spent: 12,600 years.*

Time saved using Google: Around 12,600 years, give or take a minute.

10. Google Cookin' a Lemon Chicken

Tara Calishain is the author of an online search journal called *ResearchBuzz*, and she's also the co-author of the fun book "Google Hacks." On her website, she shows off a tool (www.55fun.com/10) that helps you cooking with Google. That's right – all you need to do is enter a couple of ingredients, and you will get fitting recipes. Tara told me she's not a very good cook and uses this tool to explore new ways to combine the contents of her fridge.

Let's try this by entering *chicken lemon*, and hitting the "Grab a recipe" button. You will now be referred to a Google result page with different pages containing recipes. The actual search query that is being used is the following:

chicken lemon (inurl:allrecipes.com | inurl:epicurious | inurl:recipesource | site:cooking.com | inurl:Recipezaar)

To explain, the "inurl" operator means that only pages which have this text in their web address appear in the result, like "AllRecipes.com." The "|" operator means "or" (either the ingredients will be on *AllRecipes.com*, **or** they will be found on *Cooking.com*, or ...). The words "chicken" and "lemon" must be included, because by default Google uses the "and" operator.

So what do we get to cook then with these two ingredients? Quite a lot actually, as nearly 2 million recipes have been found! I'll pick the first one, "Roast Chicken With Lemon and Thyme." This is the full ingredients list, and you can see it indeed contains chicken and lemon:

    3 tablespoons minced fresh thyme
    2 tablespoons extra-virgin olive oil
    5 garlic cloves, chopped
    2 teaspoons grated lemon peel
    1 7-pound roasting chicken
    1 lemon, quartered
    1/4 cup dry white wine
    1 cup (about) canned low-salt chicken broth
    2 teaspoons all purpose flour

11. Douglas Adams and the Google Calculator

The Google calculator is included in Google.com's normal web search. So instead of entering words you want to find in web pages, you can simply enter math queries like the following:

*10 + 7 * 3 – 12*

The Google result will then display the solution: "10 + (7 * 3) - 12 = 19." That's already a little more fun than using a normal calculator (and incredibly helpful too, at times), but there's much more to it. Let's start with an Easter Egg – a hidden function within a program that makes it do something unexpected and interesting – and enter the following:

answer to life, the universe and everything

Entering this will result in the Google calculator showing you the answer "42." This is a reference to a mythical number from Douglas Adams' sci-fi opera "The Hitchhiker's Guide to the Galaxy." I won't spoil its meaning here, but instead suggest you simply read this great book (or, watch the movie). This isn't the only connection between Google and Douglas Adams, by the way. Completely coincidentally, the word "Googleplex" – the name the Google employees gave their California headquarters – appeared in the *Hitchhiker's Guide*:

> "And are you not," said Fook leaning anxiously forward, "a greater analyst than the Googleplex Star Thinker in the Seventh Galaxy of Light and Ingenuity which can calculate the trajectory of every single dust particle throughout a five-week Dangrabad Beta sand blizzard?"

The calculator fun doesn't stop there. The following are just some more examples of what's possible, and often these different queries can be combined to larger formulas:

seconds in a year (result: 31,556,926 seconds)

15 USD in EUR (12.74 Euro)

*120 pounds * 2000 feet in Calories* (77.77 kilocalories)

furlongs per fortnight (0.000166309524 m / s)

speed of light in knots (582,749,918 knots)

12. Oops, I Googled Again

Brian Mingus and a bunch of his friends were sitting together one evening, and after a few glasses of Italian wine, decided to write up a giant list of catch-phrases, movie titles, proverbs and random quotes... which all had to include the word "Google." Here's the list[1]... can you guess all the sources?

How many Googles must a man walk down?
Googlemorgen America
Thus quothe the raven, "Google more!"
Wherefore art thou, Google
Google and prejudice
Once upon a midnight dreary, while I Googled weak and weary
I am a Googlevangelist
Googles up, hang ten!
Google is the dictator that everyone loves
You can't spell God without Google
Stairway to Google
Dude, where's my Google?
Got Google?
We are all Googlers under Google
In the beginning, there was Google
I Google, therefore I am
It was the best of Googles, it was the worst of Googles
All my kingdom for a Googler
Peace, Love, and Google
All you need is Google
Google like it's 1999
The Google at the end of the rainbow
We've found a witch! Can we Google her?
The Googler on the roof
One flew over the Googlenest
Why can't the English teach their children how to Google
We are the knights who say Google
Google spoke Zarathustra
That's why the Google is a tramp
Murder she Googled
Save the last Google for me
There's not enough Google in this town for the both of us
I'll Google you on the flip-side
The Scarlett Google
The Purloined Google
"Googligans Island"
All my Googles

The Googlebury Tales
Google and the Beast
A Midsummer Nights' Google
20,000 Googles Under the Sea
Something Googled this way comes
Google to the death!
You smell like a Google...and you look like one too
I dream of Google
Google it again Sam
Uncle Google wants you!
To Google Times
Out of the Google and into the fire!
Don't throw the Google out with the bathwater
Bad Brian, you must say 20 hail Googles!
Bless those who Google you
Google, the final frontier
Google, interrupted
Gone with the Google
I can't get no Googlefaction
Saturday night Google
DONOTTHINKABOUTAPINKGOOGLE
You Google my name, and you know wherever I am.
Jack, I'm Googling!
I'm Gooooogling in the rain
Google outside the box
Beyond Google and evil
Do you know where your Google is?
Dr. Strangelove, or how I learned to stop worrying and love the Google
Murder by Google
To Google or not to Google.
To sleep, perchance to Google!
My name is Google, you killed my father.
It's a bird, it's a plane, it's Google!
And they Googled happily ever after
Do you promise to love, honor, and Google, until death do you part?
The lone Googler
Big Google is watching you
Google the man!
The first rule of Google is not to talk about Google
Gone with the Google
Frankly my dear, I don't give a Google!
Googleblanca
Love in the time of Google
War and Google
Googleonia
The west side Google
Larry, Moe, and Google
Give me Google or give me death!
Four Googles and 20 years ago
Googletrek, the next generation
Googlescene investigation
Red, white, and Google
Google Potter
How many Googles does it take to turn into a lightbulb?

I was lost, but now am Googled
Not a creature was Googling, not even a mouse
Do the Googlewoogy
And I took the road less Googled, and that has made all the difference
The Googler's Guide to the Galaxy
So long, and thanks for all the Google
Google No. 5
Return of the Google
Do the hokey pokey, and Google all around
Abandon all hope, all ye who Google here
A Google in the Dark
The Google that roared
Google on the Oriental Express
Googlecalifragilisticexpialidocious
You can't have your Google and eat it to
If I was the last man on earth, would you Google me?
Saved by the Google
Hand over the Google and nobody gets hurt
Google is my co-pilot
Sometimes a Google is just a Google
Do not meddle in the affairs of Googlers
Gooogle, taste the rainbow
Have you hugged your Google today?
Wake up and smell the Google
Here's a quarter; Google someone who cares
No shirt, no Google, no service
I know its only Google but I like it
If it feels good Google it
Advanced whitening Google
Keep your Googles to yourself
I think I Googled my pants
Put a Google on your face
The Googlepride Googleparade
USS Google, departing
Googlers of the world unite
Stop Googling your nose
Never underestimate the power of Google
Your Google is so soft!
Friends don't let friends Google drunk
Do you have a designated Googler?
Is that a Google in your pocket or are you just happy to see me?
The restaurant order slips these are written on are Googlebilia
All roads lead to Google
One Google, two Geegles
The Googleogical Argument
Girls giggle and boys Google
Frankly my dear, I don't give a Google.

End Notes

1. Courtesy of Brian Mingus and friends. (2004). *What would Jesus Google?* (www.55fun.com/12)

13. The Disappearing Google Logo, a Magic Trick

Any sufficiently advanced technology is indistinguishable from magic.
– Arthur C. Clarke

Here's a magic trick to surprise your friends with. What they will see is this: you are at the Google homepage, and you casually ask someone to watch the Google logo. Then, you move two of your fingers to completely cover the "o"s in the Google logo. When you remove your fingers, to much surprise, the letters "o" will be missing from the logo. Now you ask your friend to move her fingers over the missing "o"s. After your friend removes the fingers, the logo will be complete again!

The trick here? It's not really the Google homepage you and your friend are looking at – it's a fake page (darkartsmedia.com/Google.html). And when you click on the page, the letters of the logo will disappear after five seconds. Clicking again will make them reappear after five more seconds. So when you move your fingers to cover the Google logo, simply click anywhere on the page, and wait a bit before you remove your fingers… and when your friend covers the letters, you click again. (A third click, by the way, will change the page to an actual Google homepage so you can perform searches to "prove" the page is real.)

14. Fun With Google Maps, the Wiki Way

This chapter is a special one, because it wasn't written by me. In fact, it wasn't written by any single person... instead, I created a wiki (a website anyone can edit) and allowed for people to write this chapter. The topic was "Fun With Google Maps" and the result is the group-authored text that follows!

Google Maps

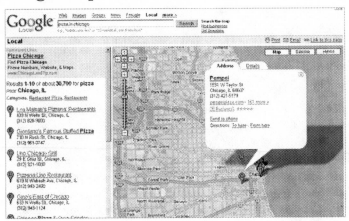

Google introduced Google Maps in February 2005 to let users "view maps, get driving directions, and search for local businesses and services." Instead of doing a multitude of things, Google Maps did only one thing (but it did that one good): show you a near full-screen map of the US – and later, other parts of the world – allowing you to drag and drop the map (or search) to get to any location. Search for *pizza in chicago*, and a couple of red pins mark the location. Clicking on a pin reveals an info box with more details on what you can find at this location.

Worldwide reach

Google Maps was originally different then Google Local, but they later merged together.

When it first launched, Google Maps was limited to just the USA, but other countries have been added to the fold, with the street level mapping of the UK and Japan being uppermost.

...and I give you the Earth!

Increasingly, even the worldwide coverage of Google Maps is insufficient for some people. Google also offers a standalone program, Google Earth, which takes the experience to an even higher level.

By offering satellite and other aerial imagery as its basis (rather than the pre-drawn maps of Google Maps), Google Earth has a far greater wow factor when simply browsing the world. It does however offer vector mapping as an overlay to the images, and allows for new data to be added to the mix via an XML data-format called KML. Innovative sites are making use of this to offer downloads of the data into Google Earth.

Mashups galore

Ever wanted to find out where your taxi is in New York city, or what the desert looks like from space? Anyone with a website, and a little programming knowledge can create their own layer on top of Google Maps. A genius move by Google, bring people in to use your maps, without having to front any programming costs. The continuous development depends on the public, just like this page.

In late June 2005, Google released its now famous API (application programming interface). It has probably become one of the most popular ones out there. Hundreds of websites are dedicated to creating "mashups," which mix Google Maps, through its API, with other kinds of data to create websites that are sometimes informative, sometimes entertaining, sometimes ridiculous, and always interesting.

One mashup, called Housing Maps (www.housingmaps.com), takes rental listings from the popular classifieds site Craigslist and adds it to Google Maps, taking a boring but useful text-based website and letting you browse it through Google's easier-to-navigate map technology. Rather browsing and clicking Craigslist's list of links, you just zoom in on a neighborhood, see where the houses are, and pick one. You can limit results by price, number of rooms, whether they accept dogs or cats, and even see pictures of the place via a simple pop-up.

The site's creator, software engineer Paul Rademacher, launched the site before Google formally announced its API, but the search giant was so impressed with his work that it soon hired him away from Dreamworks.

There are more mashups, such as Mapulator (www.mapulator.com). This tool allows you to traceroute by IP address or host name to see the path the packets take. You can run the trace from their server or from your PC. It's pretty slick, and has some settings you can tweak for doing the traceroute. It can also do "whois" queries when you click on one of the hops (to find out that hop's IP). And if you just want to know where any particular computer/server/IP is you can also type in the IP or host name in their ping tool and find out if the host is up, where it is, and get the "whois" record.

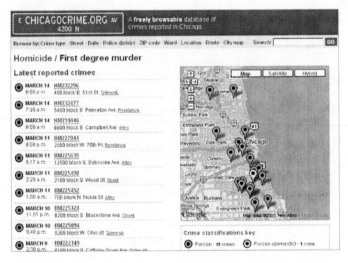

And then, if you're the paranoid type, there's Adrian Holovaty's brilliant Chicago crime map mashup at ChicagoCrime.org. It's a "freely browsable database of crimes reported in Chicago," as the site claims. You can select the type of crime you want to locate (like "armed violence" or "assault"), as well as the date range it happened, and when you click "update map," a few dozen colored pins will appear. Clicking on any pin reveals the details of the crime which was reported happening in just that location.

And then, there was a Google Maps game of Risk. A clever idea, but unfortunately game maker Hasbro didn't think it was so great and sent its creator a cease and desist. But the games don't end there. Another creative programmer by the name of Thomas Scott has created a multi-player cooperative game called Tripods (thomasscott.net/tripods/) in which users join together to protect Manhattan from the invading Tripods.

You can use the New York On Tap bar and subway map (newyorkontap.com/Subways.asp) to find great hotspots in the City That Never Sleeps, and then, since you'll be in no condition to drive, the map also shows you the nearest subway station.

If you're looking for a date, you can consult Hot or Not's database (hotmaps.frozenbear.com) and see the pictures of people who are hot (or not) in your area… all put onto Google Maps.

Are you a runner? Or do you want to know how long your hike was the other day? You can use the Gmaps Pedometer (gmap-pedometer.com) to digitally retrace your steps, and there's even the option to send a permalink of your route to somebody else.

And saving you from a potentially embarrassing situation, there's Urinal.net (urinal.net/google_map.html), which will help you find a place to do your business anywhere in the United States.

Goocam World Map (butterfat.net/goocam/) is a Google map of unprotected/open camera streams obtained from Google searches, mostly from Europe and US.

A more whimsical application is Santa Stars (www.santastars.com) which plots Christmas Light displays worldwide and allows Internet surfers to vote/comment on them.

Authors: Grimmthething, Nathan Weinberg, Omid Aladini, Mark Berry, Ryan Singel, AC Zimi, Kyle K., Ionut Alex. Chitu, Aaron Wall and Esben Fjord.

A Pac-man crop-circle spotted on Google Maps!

15. Dave Gorman's Googlewhack

Dave Gorman is a comedian who goes to great lengths to get material for his show and books – in fact, he would probably go to *any length* to get material. And that includes traveling around the world meeting complete strangers because of a truly wacky (and fun) idea. But let's start at the beginning, with a seemingly innocent email Dave received.

Dave, 31, and possibly in an early mid-life crisis, wanted to write a novel. I guess it wasn't real writer's block that kept him from doing so: it was his computer. Dave in his show tells of a truly life-changing incident:

> "Jake [the publisher] lied to me. Jake said it's just you, your imagination, and your computer. That's *not* strictly speaking true! My computer is attached to the internet. The internet contains *everything in the whole wide world ever*. I don't know about you, but I find *everything in the whole wide world ever* to be a bit distracting! I would sit there at the computer thinking… Right, here we go, Chapter one! Aahhhh…. just as soon as I've checked my email!"

Dave continues to tell that he receives more emails than he could ever read – not just from friends, family and colleagues, but complete strangers as well. One of these emails in particular captured his attention. The email contained very little, and even less that Dave *understood*. All it read was:

G'day Dave,

Did you know you're a Googlewhack?

Steve

No, as a matter of fact, Dave *didn't* know! But a little explanation is necessary in case you never heard of the word "googlewhack." In a nut-shell, a Googlewhack happens whenever you enter two words into Google and you receive *exactly one result*. A Google result containing not two, nor a thousand, and not zero, but exactly a single web page. Now there are some more rules to it – your words must be contained in a dictionary, and the result pages themselves may not be dictionaries – but that's about it. And in case you never tried, scoring a Googlewhack is not as simple as it sounds (there are websites dedicated to nothing else but googlewhacking, and listing those who found a Googlewhack first [www.googlewhack.com]).

So when Dave was informed that he himself in fact was a "Googlewhack," he was stunned. The explanation, as he later got to understand, was that one of Dave's own web pages contained those two words someone else had entered to score a Googlewhack. Of all the pages in the whole wide world! What might be even more improbable: when Dave met with googlewhacking stranger Steve a while later in London, Steve ended up trying to find a new googlewhack on Dave's computer, and found one on a page *owned by a friend of Dave* who lived in France. Dave says this struck him as an incredibly fascinating coincidence, "since there are three billion sites on Google, and I don't have three billion friends."[1]

And then, Dave caught the Googlewhack fever. Several googlewhacks and a crazy bet with his friend from France later, Dave went on a mission around the world to hunt googlewhack page owner after page owner. How that works? Simple: Dave considered himself to be a person who was found by a perfect stranger via a Googlewhack. Now he wanted to know if he could continue finding others via a Googlewhack all the same, and he aimed to do so in 10 successions before his next birthday. He would look up the contact address contained on a web page at which he found a Googlewhack, and would then travel trying to meet this person (via airplane, taxi, train or whatever mode of transportation it would take). He would then ask this person to try out to score a Googlewhack herself, and if that would be successful, he would continue traveling to the person found on that new Googlewhack page.

While the *concept* of Dave's Googlewhack adventure may sound simple, executing it wasn't. First of all, not every page Dave found contained a contact address. Also, not everyone wanted to meet him, or googlewhack for him. And there was a good chance that person, even though willing to help out, *wasn't able* to find another Googlewhack. All in all, as Dave puts it, "Googlewhacking has taken me around the world. Three times. I've played table tennis with a nine year old boy in Boston, and I've been way too familiar with some snakes in LA. I've met mini-drivers in North Wales and hippies in Memphis."[2] Now I won't spoil the ending, so if you want to find out if Dave was successful or if he lost this bet with his French friend, take a look at the book or fun DVD of the live show (www.55fun.com/15.1). In the meantime, you might want to try finding a Googlewhack yourself... or send Dave another email. Who knows what might happen?

End Notes

1. Barratt, A. World wide whack. (2004). (www.55fun.com/15.3)

2. Googlewhack Adventure homepage. (davegorman.com/googlewhack.htm)

16. Google Q&A

Google Q&A is a fun answer feature built directly into the Google.com web search. It answers certain questions right above the search result, so there's no need for you to visit a web page – the answers themselves are extracted from web pages.

You haven't seen this before? Give it a try by entering the following:

Albert Einstein birthday

Above the web page results there will now be a box reading:

Albert Einstein – Date of Birth: 14 March 1879

This works with a whole lot of search queries. You can even enter *Who is Clark Kent* ... and have Google reveal to you "Clark Kent is the civilian secret identity of the fictional character Superman." All of the following yield direct Questions & Answers results (note the answers are not always correct!):

Population of Germany
President of USA
President of France
Birthday of George Bush
Birthday of Albert Einstein
What is the birthday of Albert Einstein?
Who was President of the USA in 1996?
When did Isaac Asimov die?
Isaac Asimov date of birth
Isaac Asimov birthday
What is the birthplace of Bono?
Bono birth place
Who is Prime Minister of England?
Where is the Eiffel tower
Where is the Statue of Liberty
When was Star Wars released?
Who is the Queen of the United Kingdom?
Who wrote the Hitchhiker's Guide to the Galaxy
Catch-22 author

Permutated Sentences

Before Google's Q&A feature, a fun way to find instant facts was to move around the words of a question sentence until you hit on an answer. To explain, let's say your question is "When was Albert Einstein born?" We remove the first word, "when". We'll now do a search for the several possible rearrangements of the words, and check the Google page count for each:

- "Albert was Einstein born" (0 results)

- "born was Albert Einstein" (0 results)

- **"Albert Einstein was born" (17,500 results)**

- "Albert was born Einstein" (5 results)

... and so on.

The one phrase search of these returning the most results is our "fact finder." In this case it would almost certainly be "Albert Einstein was born", and the continuation of this sentence contains our answer. This can be automated, but takes a while as going through all permutations requires many Google searches. FindForward's "Ask Question" search (findforward.com/?t=answer) returns the following answer (you can see there are some left-overs from the snippet which aren't meaningful in this context):

> **1879, Albert Einstein was born** on March 14, 1879 German born American physicist who developed the special and general theories of relativity.

17. Celebrate Google Non-Weddings, and More

Christophe Bruno is surely having fun with Google, in his own ways. He's an artist, and many of his projects are based on the internet – and Google. In 2002 he released the "Google AdWords Happening" onto the world. AdWords are Google's small advertisement boxes displayed next to search results.... and Christophe used (or abused) them to show nonsensical messages like "mary !!!/ I love you/ come back/ john."

Also in 2002, Christophe created the *Non-Wedding page* (unbehagen.com/non-weddings/). Don't expect to necessarily understand its purpose – it's art. You can enter any two names into its two boxes, like "Peter" and "Mary," and click "Celebrate a non-wedding" on the top of the page. What happens then? Well, based on the names you entered, Christophe will simply load two different images via Google Images. Like here:

Spelling Words With Google Images Letters

This isn't the only way to combine Google images in interesting ways. You can also try to create a word by searching for its letters. For example, when you want to spell "Hello," you search for *"letter h", "letter e"*, and so on (including quotes), and always take the first image which displays the respective letter. If a letter is repeated, you choose the second image. Here's the result for spelling "Hello" with Google image results:

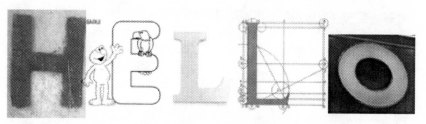

Create a Google Rebus

Instead of spelling words by their letters, you can also "spell" words by their individual parts. This makes for a good riddle to present to someone. For example, when you want to spell "lovesick" you search for "love" and "sick" and put the two result images next to each other; your friend then should guess what the word means.

Other words for this "Google Rebus" game include: "walkman," "stronghold," or "happiness." (Search for "happy" and "ness" – the first part will result in a happily laughing baby, the second in the monster from Loch Ness!)

The Google Images Storyteller

Want to turn complete paragraphs into visuals? You can, with the Google Images Storyteller (blog.outer-court.com/story/). You type a sentence – a poem, or song lyrics, or anything else – into the input box, hit submit, and it will automatically search Google Images to create a story made up of visuals only.

18. Design Your SketchUp Dream House

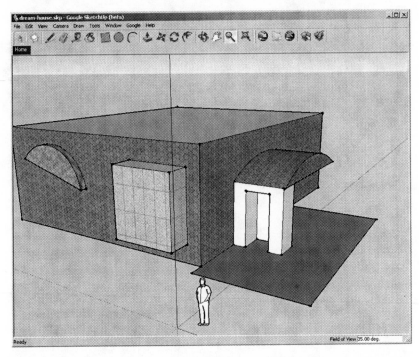

Google SketchUp is a 3D tool for creating architecture and other 3D models. Architects like it to prototype buildings, but the software is so easy to use that anyone can have fun with it. After you download SketchUp (sketchup.google.com) and follow through a hands-on tutorial (which might take you as little as 15-30 minutes) you are ready to go and design your own house. And why not make it your dream house?

Now this part of the book will live online: Send the SketchUp file of your finished dream house to philipp.lenssen@gmail.com, include your name, location, and a small description of your house and your creation will appear on **www.55fun.com/house/**

19. Kevin Bacon and the Google Network

You probably heard of the Six Degrees of Kevin Bacon game. The objective is to find a way to get from any actor to Kevin Bacon in six steps or less. For example, Sean Connery has a Bacon number of 2 (Sean Connery was in *Wrong Is Right* with Myron Natwick, who was in *Cavedweller* with Kevin Bacon). That's possible because Kevin Bacon stars in a whole lot of movies. But is he really the center of Hollywood?

I tried to find out if Kevin Bacon's network is indeed as dense as the Six Degrees game suggests. And of course, I used Google for that. Here's what I did, and you can try the same; I picked a list of 50 random famous actors, including Kevin Bacon, and searched Google trying to find out if any two of the actors on the list were in a movie together. Of course, this isn't statistical correct proof. But it's fun. Here's an example of a search query:

"Sean Connery and Julia Roberts" OR "Julia Roberts and Sean Connery" -degrees

This will return all pages with either the first or second phrase in them. (I exclude pages with the word "degrees" because I don't want to hit on pages where people played the Six Degrees game, as that would give Kevin Bacon an unfair advantage.) Whenever over 500 results have been found, I will count this as a "hit."

The following map shows all hits combined into a social network[1]. Some actors of the 50 I included in the game actually didn't make the list because they had no connection at all – like Humphrey Bogart.

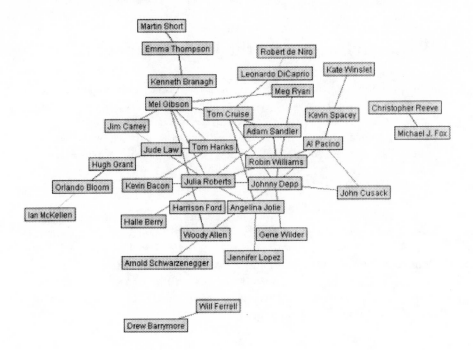

What does the map show? For one thing, that Kevin Bacon is not the center of the Hollywood universe – at least not using this (non-representative) sample. Instead, Julia Roberts, Johnny Depp and Tom Cruise seem to be the most connected. On the other hand, you can also see that it's easy for almost everyone on the list to get to Kevin Bacon in six steps or less.

A Network of Everything

How well does this approach of visualizing a network fare with something other than actors? We can also use it to find connections between any two things. For example, we can create a network of connections between things and their categories. To create the following image, I used the words *Britney Spears, apple, horse, speakers, piano, violin, carrot,* and *orange.* As categories I used *food, actor, movie, book, song, album, company, band, tool* and a few more. I applied a threshold of 50 Google results to count something as connection, and I used glue phrases like "is a", "are an" and so on:

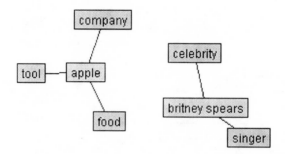

You can see Britney Spears is a celebrity singer. "Apple" is an ambiguous term, meaning both the company, and the fruit.

End Notes

1. The visuals are created using Sun's GraphLayout tool.

20. The Google Alphabet

Can you guess the top Google search result for the letters of the alphabet? For example, when you search for "a", the top Google result is Apple Computer Inc (naturally, the top result changes over time). Simply note down the first company, organization, software, person or product you can think of below:

A: *Apple Computer Inc*
B: _____
C: _____
D: _____
E: _____
F: _____
G: _____
H: _____
I: _____
J: _____
K: _____
L: _____
M: _____
N: _____
O: _____
P: _____
Q: _____
R: _____
S: _____
T: _____
U: _____
V: _____
X: _____
Y: _____
Z: _____

Solution

Apple Computer Inc, B'Tselem, C-SPAN, D-Link, E! Online, F-Secure, Gmail, H-Net, iTools, Jennifer Lopez, K Desktop Environment, Council of Europe portal, Texas A&M University, SBC Knowledge Network Explorer, O'Reilly Media, PFLAG.org, Q4music.com, The R Project for Statistical Computing, McDonald's, T-Mobile, whatUseek Web Search, V-Day, President George W. Bush, X.Org, Yahoo! Messenger, Z Communications. *(This is from 2005 – results often change.)*

21. Google Search Tips

How do you have more fun when searching? Simply: become a better searcher. Here are some syntax basics as well as advanced tricks or bits of trivia for searching with Google.com:

A quote/ phrase search can be written with both quotations *"like this"* as well as a minus (or dot) in-between words, *like-this.*

Google didn't always understand certain special characters like "#", but now it does; a search for *C#*, for example, yields meaningful results. Note that not every character works yet.

Google allows 32 words within the search query (some years ago, only up to 10 were used, and Google ignored subsequent words). You rarely will need so many words in a single query – *just thinking of such a long query is a hard thing to do, as this sentence with twenty words shows.* However, it can come in handy for advanced or automated searching.

You can find synonyms of words. E.g. when you search for *house* but you want to find "home" too, search for *~house.* To get to know which synonyms the Google database stores for individual words, simply use the minus operator to exclude synonym after synonym. Like this: *~house -house -home -housing -floor*

Google has a lesser known "numrange" operator which can be helpful. Using e.g. *2000..2006* (that's two dots in-between two numbers) will find 2000, 2001, 2002 and so on until 2006.

Google's "define" operator allows you to look up word definitions. For example, *define:nasa* yields "National Aeronautics and Space Administration" along with many more explanations. You can also enter *what is nasa* for similar results.

Google searches for all of your words, whether or not you write a "+" before them. Therefore, writing queries *+like +this* is not really necessary.

Sometimes, Google seems to understand "natural language" queries and shows you so-called "onebox" results. This happens for example when you enter *goog, weather new york, ny, war of the worlds* (for this one, movie times, move ratings and other information will show), or *beatles* (which yields an instant discography).

Not all Googles are the same! Depending on your country, Google might forward you to a different version of Google with potentially different results to the same query. For example in Germany and France, certain results are censored for a long time now. In early 2006, Google decided to self-censor Chinese search results (such as web pages of human rights organizations) in compliance with Chinese government requests – which not only resulted in an oddly skewed Google.cn, but also a public outcry from both diehard fans and organizations such as Reporters Without Borders.

For some search queries, Google uses its own search result advertisement system to offer jobs. Try entering *work at google* and sometimes, you find job offers straight from Google.

Some say that whoever turns up first for the search query *president of the internet* is, well, the President of the internet. Take a look at the results for this search to find out who's currently ruling you!

Can you guess why the Disney homepage is in a top 10 search result position when you enter "Exit", "No", or "Leave" into Google? Try it out, you'll be surprised (I won't spoil here why this is happening, but it has something to do with adult websites).

Google doesn't have "stop words" anymore. Stop words traditionally are words like "the", "or" and similar which search engines tended to ignore. Nowadays, Google includes all of your words, even the former stop words.

You can use the wildcard character "*" in phrases. This is helpful for finding song texts – let's say you forgot a word or two, but you remember the gist, as in *"love you twice as much * oh love * *."* You can even use the wildcard character without searching for anything specific at all, as in this search: "* * * * * * *."

The following search tip, on the other hand, you better not follow. But you may sing along…

When it's late at night
And you've an essay due
And you don't know what to write
I'll tell you what to do
Before sunrise
Find something to plagiarize

on Google
Talkin' 'bout Google.."
— Mort, The Google Song

22. Googlepark

Following is *Googlepark: Scoble goes to Google* (www.55fun.com/22) courtesy of Jamie Grant (Robert Scoble is a Microsoft employee with a popular blog).

23. Googleshare

Googleshare (also called mindshare) is one of the most powerful approaches to have fun with mining the web for data, and answers. Here's how it works; when you enter a single term or phrase into Google, you get a certain page count. For example, you enter *"Rolling Stones"* as phrase search and Google tells you there are about 10,500,000 pages on the web containing this phrase. Now you combine this query with one of the Rolling Stones singers, searching for: *"Rolling Stones" "Mick Jagger"*

This results in 1,470,000 pages. The percentage the second value has in relation to the first is its "googleshare." So Mick Jagger has a googleshare of 14% with the Rolling Stones. This is very high; Keith Richards only has a Rolling Stones googleshare of 5%. This makes Mick Jagger the most popular in the band. Peter Smith, on the other hand, has a googleshare of only 0.006% with the Stones – because he's not a band member, of course.

Here are some more googleshare examples:

Full House:

Ashley Olsen	1.46%
John Stamos	1.07%
Bob Saget	1.04%
Mary-Kate Olsen	0.97%
Dave Coulier	0.58%
Jodie Sweetin	0.56%

Tom Cruise:

Nicole Kidman	20.80%
Katie Holmes	16.34%
Penelope Cruz	7.51%
Mimi Rogers	0.57%

Harrison Ford:

Star Wars	14.97%
Firewall	8.98%
Blade Runner	4.06%
Raiders of the Lost Ark	2.78%
The Fugitive	2.12%
Indiana Jones and the Last Crusade	1.43%
American Graffiti	1.13%
Six Days Seven Nights	0.9%
Regarding Henry	0.55%
The Mosquito Coast	0.5%

We can also find the googleshare for a specific year and an event. For example, we can determine the googleshare for 1950 and "Disco," 1951 and "Disco," and so on for all years until 2005. We then normalize this data by taking into account that some years are represented more often on the web (for example, the year 1960 on its own appears more often than the year 1961). What we get as result is a peak year which shows us when this fad or person was on the height of its fame, or when an event happened. I've created a tool called "Centuryshare" as part of the FindForward search engine (findforward.com/?t=century) which helps visualize this data:

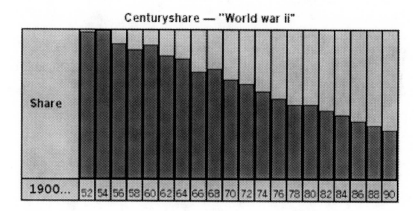

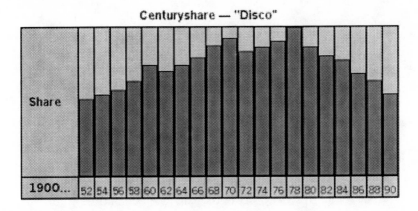

As you can see, you can determine the googleshare for anything and everything, really. Douwe Osinga, who currently works at Google Zürich, created a project called "Land Geist" (see www.55fun.com/23.2 – back then Douwe actually used search engine AllTheWeb, not Google, to compile his data). Land Geist features different maps for different words, like "holiday," "rice" or "poverty." The most popular countries for holidays according to Land Geist are Mauritius, Cyprus and Spain. Determining the "countryshare" for "Islam," on the other hand, returns Saudi Arabia, Afghanistan and Iran as top contenders.

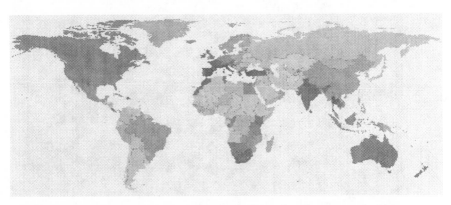

The "countryshare" map for the term "holiday" (the darker the country, the higher its googleshare). Courtesy of Douwe Osinga.

24. The Shortest Google Search (and the One Returning the Most Results)

Can you find the **shortest Google search** that *doesn't* return any results, using only the letters a-z (no Umlaute or accented characters) and the numbers 0-9? How many letters will you need? For example, you can enter "d8" into Google. It's only two letters, so it's very short. But whoops – it returns nearly 5 million pages! Or search for "njd2we9e2." That returns no results... but it's also 9 letters long. Can you make a short search with no pages at all found on the web?

Answer: _____

Page count: _____

Also, can you find the **Google search returning the most results?** You are allowed to use any character at all (not only letters from a-z and numbers). Let's say you search for *Beatles*. More than 16 million results. Not bad already. Or search for *USA*. That'll be over 1 billion result pages, as Google tells you. That's better, but you can go even higher than that. Which single search query finds the most result pages?

Answer: _____

Page count: _____

25. Google Rotated and Mini Google

"Mini Me, if I ever lost you I don't know what I would do. (pauses)
I would probably move on, get another clone but there would be a 15
minute period there where I would just be inconsolable."
– Dr. Evil, Austin Powers: The Spy Who Shagged Me

Both of the following fun ways to browse Google need the Internet
Explorer browser, so feel free to skip this chapter if you're using
Firefox or any browser other than Internet Explorer.

Google Rotated (blog.outer-court.com/rotated/) shows you the normal,
actual Google (with all of its functionalities)... except that everything's
rotated 180°. Including the Google homepage, the search results, and
even the web pages you click on in the results. When people visit
Google Rotated they're usually either trying to adjust their monitor, or
bend their neck leftwards.

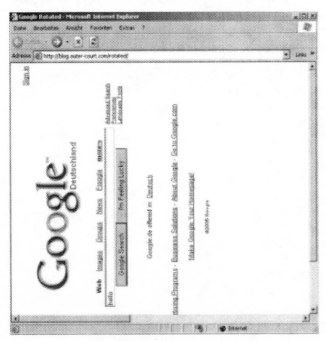

Google Rotated... it's another way to look at search.

Mini Google (blog.outer-court.com/mini.html), on the other hand, doesn't make you bend your neck. Then again, it may make you move your face really, really close to the screen... 'cause it's tiny. About the size of your thumbnail. Good luck searching for something with Mini Google, and good luck hitting on a search result page – as a bonus, if you managed to do that the page you clicked on will be mini too!

Google Mini. Small, but fun!

26. The Google Quiz: How Much Do You Know About Google?

Are you a Google expert? Do you know everything about the company and its services? Or are you still new to the topic, and you only used their search engine for a couple of times so far? Well, you can put your knowledge to the test in this quiz which will answer the question: How much do you know about Google? Get a pencil and cross the single right answer for every question, and calculate your score afterwards.

1. Google Inc. was founded in ...

a) 1996
b) 1998
c) 2000

2. Google Inc. was founded by ...

a) Sergey Page and Larry Brin
b) Eric Schmidt and Larry Page
c) Larry Page and Sergey Brin

3. Which search operator does Google enable by default?

a) The AND operator
b) The OR operator
c) The NOT operator

4. Google once used Yahoo's search result to feed its engine. True?

a) Yes, from 1998-2000.
b) No, it was the other way round – Yahoo used Google once.
c) No, Google and Yahoo never had any search relationship.

5. Google Analytics is a service to ...

a) Check if your web pages validate
b) Check how many people visit your web pages
c) Check your Google PageRank

6. In 2006, Eric Schmidt is Google's ...

a) Vice President Engineering
b) Eric left the company in 2004 to pursue his hobbies
c) Chief Executive Officer

7. What was the name of the search engine the Google founders developed before Google?

a) PageRanker
b) BackRub
c) Gogol

8. What is the algorithm behind Google's PageRank?

a) The more pages link to you (and the higher their PageRank), the higher your page's PageRank
b) You get 1 PageRank point for every web page you own
c) The algorithm behind PageRank is kept secret, similar to the Coca-Cola formula

9. Why do some sites get "banned" from the Google index?

a) They tried methods to get their pages ranked better which Google considers spam
b) They have content which is illegal in this state/ country
c) Both a) and b) are true.

10. At which university did the Google founders meet?

a) Oxford University
b) MIT
c) Stanford University

11. What is the "Googleplex"?

a) It's where Google employees work
b) It's a solar system which shares only the name with Google.com
c) It's the server farm Google built up to deliver search results to you

12. Which words are printed on the Froogle homepage?

a) Search for any product you want (or discover new ones).
b) froo·gle (fru'gal) n. Smart shopping through Google.
c) Froogle. Just shopping.

13. Around how many hits do you get for the word "Hello" (in 2006)?

a) 420,000 pages
b) 420,000,000 pages
c) 42,000,000,000 pages

14. If you want to find a place to grab a pizza, you go to ...

a) Google Food
b) Google Places
c) Google Local

15. At the Association of National Advertisers annual conference in October 2005, who said Google will take 300 years to fulfill its mission to index the world's data?

a) Eric Schmidt
b) Larry Page
c) Marissa Mayer

16. What colors do the letters of the Google logo have, from left to right?

a) Red – Blue – Green – Yellow – Green
b) Blue – Red – Yellow – Blue – Green – Red
c) Blue – Yellow – Purple – Yellow – Red – Blue

How well did you do?

Calculate your points by adding 10 points for each question you answered like the following: *1 - b, 2 - c, 3 - a, 4 - b, 5 - b, 6 - c, 7 - b, 8 - a, 9 - c, 10 - c, 11 - a, 12 - a, 13 - b, 14 - c, 15 - a, 16 – b.*

0–50 points: Though you have a mild interest in Google, you're new to the topic. Maybe you prefer other search engines, or you're not using the web for a lot of tasks. You have yet to learn how to become a power searcher, but you're on your way.

60–110 points: You already understand more than just the basics of how Google works. Using your search power, you can locate almost anything you want. You are likely making good use of Gmail, Google News, and other Google services.

120–160 points: Consider yourself a Google guru. In fact, with your knowledge you could write a book like this. Chances are you are reading a lot of news articles on Google, and you know the ins and outs of its services. You probably use Google on a daily basis for many years now.

27. Recreate Google From Memory

Before you flip to the next pages, try something: take pen and paper, and recreate Google from memory. Try to sketch every link and other detail from the Google homepage just as you remember it. When you're done, take a look at what some other people created faced with the same task – and then finally take a look at the actual Google homepage!

Which parts of the Google homepage did you get right, and which did you get wrong – and can you imagine why?

By Jordan Hamer

By Jack Hynes

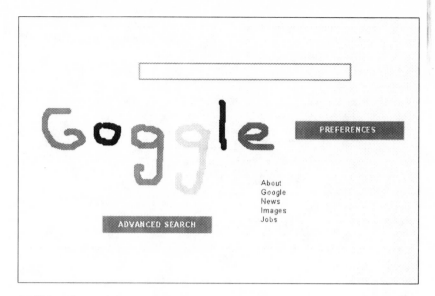

By ¥€$... I got a feeling the artist wasn't motivated!

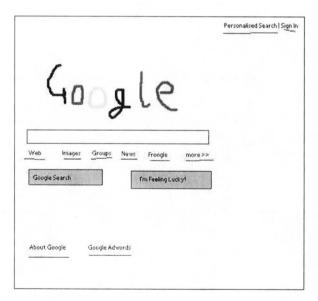

By Splasho

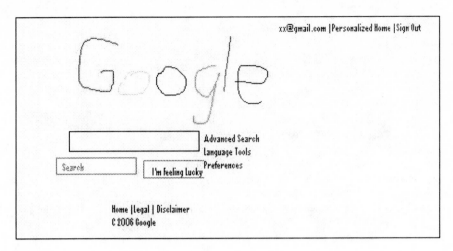

By Joe

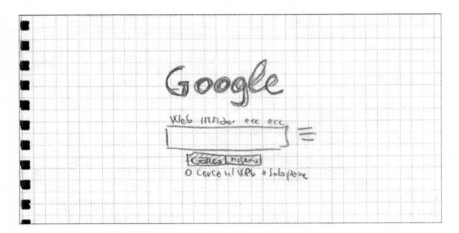

By Luka

28. The Strange World of Google News

Google News is Google's automated news polling machine. It will display whatever it thinks is important today based on what other news sources write. The fact that it's automated may make it more objective (even though the included sites are still picked manually, and in the case of China, the local government has a word to say in it too), but at times, the Google machines get it wrong. They put the false image next to a news story, or the snippet doesn't fit with the headline – or the story's a hoax, like when Google News in November 2003 announced that Google Inc had been bought by food giant Nestlé ("Nestlé says Google will be renamed NesGoogle and have a recipe section added to its main page"). I've collected some of the examples of the past here – it's good the Google computers don't have human feelings, because they sure would feel guilty now.

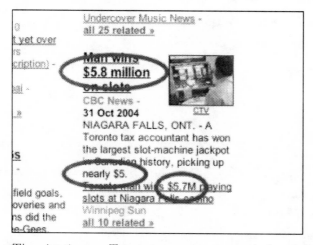

The snippet[1] says a Toronto tax accountant won the largest slot-machine jackpot in Canadian history – $5!

Exorcist resurrected at US box office
Guardian - **2 hours ago**
Exorcist: The Beginning scared its way to the top of the American box office this weekend, surprising industry observers by taking a better than expected $18.
Exorcist Bedevils Alien's Box Office People Magazine (subscription)
Newest 'Exorcist' riddled with problems Bangor Daily News
Screendaily.com (subscription) - Rediff - The Malaysia Star - BBC News - **all 298 related »**

The Exorcist prequel from 2004 made $18 on the opening weekend.[2] That's even better than winning a $5 lottery jackpot!

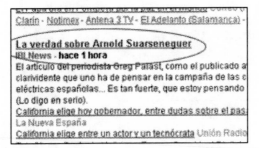

Clarin · Notimex · Antena 3 TV · El Adelanto (Salamanca) ·

La verdad sobre Arnold Suarseneguer
IBL News - **hace 1 hora**
El artículo del periodista Greg Palast, como el publicado a clarividente que uno ha de pensar en la campaña de las e eléctricas españolas... Es tan fuerte, que estoy pensando (Lo digo en serio).
California elige hoy gobernador, entre dudas sobre el pas
La Nueva España
California elige entre un actor y un tecnócrata Unión Radio

Who is Arnold Suarseneguer? (From Google News Spain in October 2003[3].)

This interesting headline[1] is the top news for Google in July, 2005!

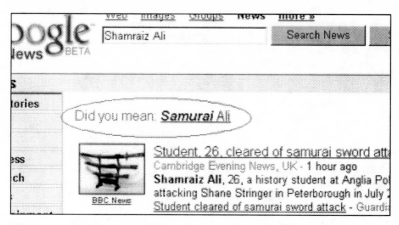

"Did you mean: Samurai Ali?"²

The photo next to the headline "Floriday Keys to welcome tourists" shows a flooded area. Kenny⁵ says, "I'd wait for the water to go down first..."

Is it coincidence that Steve Jobs and the chimpanzee use similar gestures?[6]

A refreshingly personal view on today's news[2]...

Schlagzeilen

Deutscher und Niederländer in Irak getötet

NDR Online - vor 10 Stunden gefunden

Bei einem Anschlag im Irak sind zwei Mitarbeiter einer Bremer Pumpenbaufirma getötet worden. Das bestätigte ein Sprecher der Bremer Innenbehörde am Dienstag. Bei den Opfern handelt es sich um einen Deutschen und einen Niederländer. Nach Informationen ...

Ein Deutscher und e

This headline and snippet[7] from Google News Germany suggest that a German has been killed in Iraq. Formula 1 driver Michael Schumacher shown to the right is German, but he's also alive.

Google duo move up on Forbes' list

Times of India, India - 20 hours ago

NEW YORK: **Google** Inc's mammoth initial public offering has r interesting side benefit - an entry into the upper echelons of Fort

Bill Gates keeps wealthiest crown ZDNet UK

BBC News

Bill Gates is part of the Google duo?

News BETA   Search and browse 4,500 news sourc

Top Stories U.S. ⌄ Go

ories

Canadians Authorities Arrest US President Bush On War Charges

Axis of Logic - 3 hours ago

Canadian authorities have arrested US president George W. Bush in Ottawa. He has been charged with several offences under Canada's War Crimes Act.

China Daily

Bush Grateful for 'Five-Finger' Welcome Kansas City Star (subscription)

President Bush Pays Visit to Canada Los Angeles Times (subscription)

Reuters - Bloomberg - CJAD - CNN - all 984 related »

ss

ch

inment

This was the actual Google top story on December 2004 when George Bush visited Canada (Google incidentally picked up a satire piece).

News BETA   Search and browse 4,500 news sources up

Top Stories U.S. ⇕ (Go)

Senate Reaches Compromise on Sexual Filibuster
Postcards from the Pug Bus (satire) - **1 hour ago**
By Phil Maggitti. WASHINGTON - Last night fourteen members of
the Senate agreed to an historic compromise on sexual filibustering
that may have saved what one senator called "this august body" from ridicule and
irreparable harm. ...
Reid claims triumph; Ensign concerned about precedent Las Vegas Review-Journal
IT'S A COMPROMISE: SENATE ENDS IMPASSE San Jose Mercury News
OregonLive.com - Detroit Free Press - MarketWatch -
Record-Searchlight (subscription) - **all 1,893 related »**

Washington Post

Google News picks up satire, once more[8]...

World »

ABC News Attack on US Base in Mosul Kills 22
ABC News - **1 hour ago**
BAGHDAD, Iraq Dec 21, 2004 - Rockets and mortar rounds
struck a US base in the northern city of Mosul on Tuesday,
killing at least 22 people and wounding 50, a Pentagon official
said.
Europe ; Blair praises Iraqi election bravery in flying visit
Keralanext
Blair makes surprise Iraq trip Reuters
Bloomberg - WVLT - Xinhua - Zaman Online - **all 481 related »**

CBC News

*Grant Shellen, who posted this screenshot[9], says, "The importance of our punctual
friend the colon is clearly evident here, when its absence makes it seem as though
ABC News is getting a bit too aggressive in its coverage."*

Virus In Horses

NBC4i.com - **12 hours ago**
West Nile virus (WNV) is a viral disease previously seen only in Africa, Asia, and southern Europe. This virus can cause encephalitis, an infection of the brain and the spinal cord. The West Nile virus is ...

KBTV4.tv

West Nile tentatively diagnosed in Washington, last of 48

Hmmm...the picture to the right reads "Hilton."[10]

Scientists pack up: "Everything explained"

BBC News - **0.3 femtoseconds ago**
Scientists all round the world today went home for a nice cup of tea after a revolutionary breakthrough explained everything. The new unified theory (NUT) unites science and religion, explains genetics, the origin of the universe, quantum phenomena, and provides the first instant cure for a hangover in human history.

BBC News

Scientists: "It's very simple actually, very embarrassing" New Scientist
PC Pro - Mac Daily News - **and 99 related »**

OK, this one is fake! It was created as part of the "Goodle" homepage[11] *showing good news only.*

I admit it, this one's fake too. It's Paul's completely personalized Google News circa 2031, covering nothing but... Paul himself.

Health »

SARS Claims Life Of Canadian Doctor

NBC 17.com - **30 minutes ago**

TORONTO -- Although the epidemic of severe acute respiratory
syndrome is officially over, another victim has died in Canada.
MD died trying to save others' from SARS Canada.com
SARS doc inspires two sons Calgary Sun
Toronto Star - WAVY-TV - Reuters - ABS CBN News -
and 204 related »

Canada.com

8000 US doctors demand Canadian style health care

National Union of Public and General Employees -
2 hours ago

Washington - Nearly 8,000 American doctors, arguing that US
health care is collapsing, have called for a national health
insurance system similar to the one Canada has had for nearly
40 years.
Joe Crankshaw: All of a sudden, doctors warm to Clinton-style
health plan Stuart News

National Union
of Public and
General
Employees

*Sometimes, it's just the way two stories are composed side-by-side[13] which gives new
meaning not intended by either story.*

End Notes

1. Via Stéfan Sinclair. (www.stefansinclair.name)
2. Via Craig S. Cottingham. (xcom2002.com/doh/)
3. Via Caspa.tv. (www.caspa.tv)
4. Via SecurityTribune. (securitytribune.com)
5. Via Kennry. (www.55fun.com/28.5)
6. Via Eric Lebeau. (zorgloob.com)
7. Via Dr. Web. (drweb.de)
8. Flickr. (www.55fun.com/28.8)
9. Via Grant Shellen. (www.55fun.com/28.9)
10. Via Jennifer. (jennifermonk.com/blog/)
11. Goodle. (www.55fun.com/28.11)
12. Aberson. (www.55fun.com/28.12)

29. Aliens Attack Google!

Do you wish to see a full-scale alien attack take place on the Google homepage? You can! In fact, not only does Netdisaster (www.netdisaster.com) allow you to destroy Google.com, you can destroy any other web page – in a multitude of ways, too. You can send meteors, flood it, nuke it, shoot it, paintball or chainsaw it, send God onto the page, cover it with flowers, or terrify it with a horde of flies, wasps, snails, worms and dinosaurs. If you're not the aggressive type, you can also just spill some coffee on the page instead...

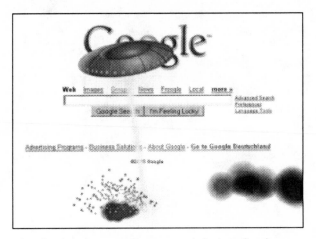

An alien laser burns semi-permanent holes into Google.com.

I asked creator Denis Rionnet from Lyon, France, how he got the idea for this tool. Denis tells me, "A few years ago, I started programming an online tool that allows users to turn any site into some African witch-doctor advertisement. ... So, people have fun with this tool and send the link to each other. But that's only for French speaking persons! So one year ago, I was wondering if I could find another idea of a tool that would interact with any site in a more visual way."

Denis goes on to say that, after making sure his idea of weapons and plagues "destroying" any target site was technically possible, he worked hard on the site hoping people would enjoy it. And it did have an effect on people, but with some surprising results.

Not everybody understands how Netdisaster works; that basically, it's just a bunch of visual effects without actual consequences for the target site. Some of the users wondered if they were staying anonymous during the attack, and also asked if the attacked site was harmed. Denis says, "Someone wrote to me once, because a site got out of order right after he had targeted it with Netdisaster – the server of this site was just down, coincidentally. He couldn't believe that Netdisaster was not to blame at all, and urged me to do something about it!"

Google is currently being flooded... the fish at the bottom seem to enjoy it.

Meteors rain down on Google...

30. Top Ten Signs You Are Addicted to Google

10. Your kids still believe the Googlebot is bringing the Christmas presents.

9. When someone asks "How are you?" you mouse-click in mid-air at them and say "I'm feeling lucky."

8. You shout at the librarian when she takes more than a tenth of a second to find your book.

7. You just lost a case in court to name your newborn son "Google."

6. Google is your second-best friend... and you're thinking maybe it should be first.

5. Your Google shirt is losing color.

4. When people talk to you, you try to optimize their keywords.

3. Your last three Sunday family trips have been to the Googleplex.

2. You are convinced "What's your PageRank?" is a good pick-up line.

And the number one sign you are addicted to Google:

1. You are completely clueless without a computer.

31. Dig a Hole Through Earth

> *"I wonder if I shall fall right through the earth! How funny it'll seem to come out among the people that walk with their heads downward! The antipathies, I think—" (she was rather glad there was no one listening, this time, as it didn't sound at all the right word) "—but I shall have to ask them what the name of the country is, you know. Please, Ma'am, is this New Zealand? Or Australia?" (and she tried to curtsey as she spoke—fancy, curtseying as you're falling through the air! Do you think you could manage it?) "And what an ignorant little girl she'll think me for asking! No, it'll never do to ask: perhaps I shall see it written up somewhere."*
> *– Lewis Carroll, Alice in Wonderland*

Have you ever wondered where you would end up if you dug a hole right through earth? Wonder no more (at least if you got an internet connection): Luís Felipe Cipriani from Brazil developed a website (www.55fun.com/31.1) based on Google Maps which lets you click on any starting point on the globe. A small info box pops up on which you can click "Dig here." Afterwards you discover the location you would come out at the other end.

I've asked my friend Justin Pfister (blog.justinpfister.com) if he knew some cool places to dig. Indeed, he did!

The only place to dig through the center of the Earth and land in China is the central west half of South America. The Upper half of Chile would be a great place to start.

What if Darwin explored downward by digging a giant hole in Galapagos? He'd end up off the coast of Sri Lanka in the Indian Ocean.

Does Stonehenge have an important location on the other side of the Earth? That depends how important you think the coast of New Zealand is.

What if everyone in the United States started digging huge holes? They would all end up in the Indian Ocean.

What if the people in Australia wanted to go "down under" too? They would all find themselves in the Northern Atlantic Ocean.

If the Lost City of Atlantis is still sinking through the center of the Earth, where might it come out? It would pop up in or around Australia. Could it be that Australia is the Lost City of Atlantis?

If Japan really starts to run out of space and begins building skyscrapers that go into the ground, they might eventually poke out near Brazil.

During the Cold War, if some people in Russia built some very deep bomb shelters, they would have ended up on the Southern Ocean near Antarctica.

What if the people in Iraq dig too deep into the Earth in search of oil? They will end up in the Pacific Ocean.

32. Googlebombing

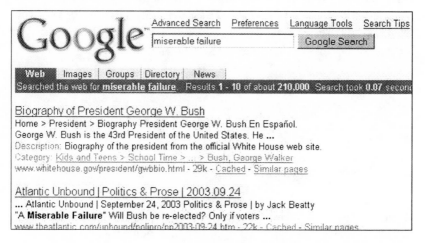

A googlebomb is when a group of people get together trying to push a site up the Google rankings... a site which seemingly doesn't belong there. To do that, they all use the same link text when linking to the specific site – trying to make Google think the words in the link are indeed relevant to the page.

Probably the most well-known "Googlebomb" was for the phrase *miserable failure*. It would lead to the official biography of President George W. Bush on the White House servers. The effect is particularly convincing when you ask people to first enter *miserable failure*, and then press the "I'm feeling lucky" button; they will be referred to the top result directly, and some even thought Google expressed political beliefs here. Of course that's not true – Google only created the algorithms that now run automatically, and from time to time, get abused to discredit people or organizations. Google's only editorial decision in cases like these is to display small disclaimers close to googlebombed search results, and educate people on what's happening. A reply posted to their official Google Blog[1] was:

> We don't condone the practice of googlebombing, or any other action that seeks to affect the integrity of our search results, but we're also reluctant to alter our results by hand in order to prevent such items from showing up. Pranks like this may be distracting to some, but they don't affect the overall quality of our search service, whose objectivity, as always, remains the core of our mission.

But the *failure* bomb against George Bush (which was quickly receiving a counter-googlebomb targeting director Michael Moore) wasn't the first one to appear on the search scene. Adam Mathes of the *Über* blog is credited with the invention of the Googlebomb. In his blog on April 6, 2001, he wrote:

> Today, uber readers, you have a chance to make history.
>
> Or at least legitimize some new jargon I'm about to make up.
>
> Today's jargon of the day is:
>
> GOOGLE BOMBING

Adam continued to explain the philosophy behind Googlebombs, which was backriding on the philosophy of Google itself:

> In a bizarre surreal bow to the power of perception on the web, what you say about a page becomes just as important as the actual content of the page. The page must be what other people say it is. That Google adheres to this rule and is by far the most effective search engine raises many interesting issues, none of which I will attempt to discuss or explicate.
>
> Now Google is smart, simply having tons of the same links with the same phrase on a single page will do nothing. It requires a multitude of pages to have that link with specific link text. But this power can be harnessed with a concentrated group effort.

Adam was only interested in pulling off a prank – a political agenda didn't have anything to do with it. So, he urged his readers to googlebomb his friend Andy Pressman with the words "talentless hack." And thus Googlebombs were born.

Of course, it didn't stop there. Not only did Googlebombs work, they were also becoming an effective tool in web propaganda.

"Weapons of mass destruction" was a Googlebomb criticizing the US Iraq politics. Because when you searched for this phrase in Google and hit the "I'm feeling lucky" button, the following page looked just like a normal "Document not found" page. But if you were to look closely, you noticed it read:

 These Weapons of Mass Destruction cannot be displayed

The weapons you are looking for are currently unavailable. The country might be experiencing technical difficulties, or you may need to adjust your weapons inspectors mandate.

Please try the following:

- Click the 🔁 Regime change button, or try again later.
- If you are George Bush and typed the country's name in the address bar, make sure that it is spelled correctly. (IRAQ).
- To check your weapons inspector settings, click the **UN** menu, and then click **Weapons Inspector Options**. On the **Security Council** tab, click **Consensus**. The settings

(A similar approach had been used as target for the words "Arabian Gulf," which returns a "The Gulf You Are Looking For Does Not Exist. Try Persian Gulf" message in the style of typical document-not-found pages.)

Yet another politically motivated Googlebomb was for "French military victories." When you clicked "I'm feeling lucky," the result page looked just like Google itself, and – mimicking the Google spelling suggestion tool – asked: "Did you mean: <u>french military</u> <u>***defeats***</u>." (In similar vein, another Googlebomb for "anti-war peace protesters" suggested "Did you mean: <u>anti-war ***violent*** protesters</u>.")

"Liar" was the word used in a Googlebomb against UK's Prime Minister. Entering it into Google brought you to a biography of Tony Blair, who was also involved in the Iraq war and, like George Bush, believed the reports on Weapons of Mass Destruction were accurate. Tony Blair was also the target of a Googlebomb campaign trying to connect the word "poodle" to him (it was less successful, but if you restrict your search to UK sites only it might still return Blair's homepage today).

Ken Jacobson's "waffles" campaign was a Googlebomb against United States Senator and Presidential candidate in 2004, John Kerry, leading to his official homepage. In response to that, Kerry supporters bought advertisements on related Google search results urging searchers to "read about President Bush's Waffles."

"Litigious bastards" was one of the more rude Googlebombs. Its target? The SCO Group, infamous for its attempt to sue companies like IBM and others who used Linux, as well as Linux users, and its claim to own intellectual property rights to the Unix operating system. As far as the campaign's target goes, the Googlebomb was a success and managed to propel the SCO homepage to a number 1 spot for the phrase "litigious bastards." As is the fate of many Googlebombs, this one has disappeared by now due to search result rankings undergoing constant changes.

"Buffone," another Googlebomb, is Italian for "clown" and was trying to make fun of Silvio Berlusconi, Italian Prime minister.

Today, there are simply too many Googlebombs around at any given time to keep track of them all. Many people try to start new ones, and only some are successful. Others manage to connect their target to the search phrase they chose, but that isn't always the hard part. In fact, for many search phrases it's trivial to make any page to be the top result in Google; this is always the case when the phrase is not competitive. However, it's not as easy to get people to react on the Googlebomb, let alone take notice. And even if people take notice, they might start to counter-googlebomb, which then turns this into a rather meaningless power game of which campaign attracts more followers to use link text as needed.

End Notes

1. The Google Blog. (www.55fun.com/32.1)

2. Über – Better than you, daily. (www.55fun.com/32.2)

33. Google Ads Gone Wrong

Google's ads are the way Google Inc makes money. They are displayed on Google search results, related Google services (like Gmail), or on any other site with a web owner trying to earn some spare change. (You can buy your own ads using "AdWords," or sell your page space using "AdSense.")

Now the key to Google's ad success was relevancy. Google analyzes what's on the page, or what the searcher is looking for, and automatically chooses a fitting advertisement.

And this is where the fun starts.

As with any automation, we can see how sometimes computers and the human-created algorithms they work on are incredibly dumb at deciding just *what fits* onto a given page... in particular on exceptional circumstances. Here's a slide-show of those exceptions:

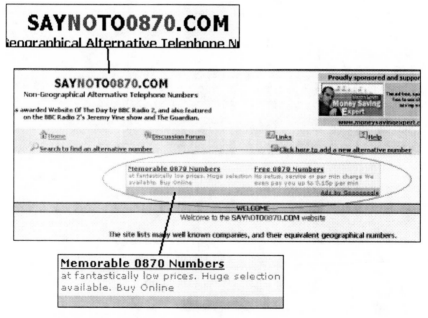

The page clearly states "Say No To 0870 Telephone Numbers." And what did the Google ads on it decide to advertise? "Memorable 0870 numbers," and "Free 0870 numbers."¹

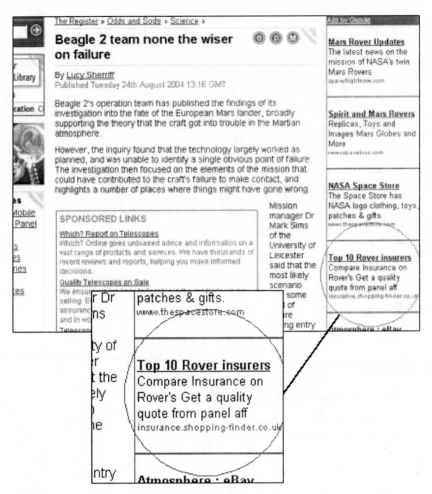

Yes, why not just insure the Mars Rover? That way, if it gets lost the mission is still a success...

The Yahoo shop has everything. Including farts reviews.

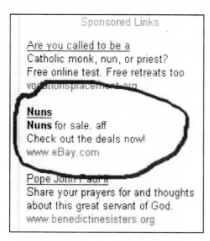

Oh, eBay has everything too![2]

Sponsored Links

Herbal Remedies
Herbal remedies and healthy teas
available at Dragonwater Tea.
dragonwater.com

Sexy **Syphilitic** Singles
Free photos, personals and hot
profiles of local singles. Free
www.infobert.com

Free eBay Success Kit
How I Earn $277,000 a Year on eBay.
Get Your Free Kit - Today Only!
Easy-Money-at-Home.Info

Syphilitic singles[3]... hmm, there has to be a bigger fish out there...

mary !!!
I love you
come back
john

This is a "performance art" ad by Christophe Bruno (see Chapter 17).

Of course there's a discount. The pet is dead after all.

Google ads can be a one-stop life help center[1]. First, they aid you on cheating; then, they help your partner find out about it; and finally, they tell you how to cope with it once that happens!

Ads by Google

Israel in a Nutshell
Learn about Israel-Palestine in a Nutshell. Books available.
www.enisen.com

Gaza Strip Singles
Meet Your Perfect Match! and Stay Connected.
gdconnect.net/dating

Jerusalem Israel Sale
New & used Jerusalem Israel. aff Check out the deals now!
www.eBay.com

What's that...?

Sponsored Links

Kryptonite
Huge selection
Low prices guaranteed!
www.ridegear.com
Interest: ▆▆▆▆

Kryptonite
Find the best deal! Compare prices
on all products from across the web
www.mysimon.com
Interest: ▆▆▆▆

This might come in handy when Superman's around.

End Notes

1. Xcom 2002. (xcom2002.com/doh/)

2. Colleen Kane. (www.55fun.com/33.2)

3. Harlow. (acsu.buffalo.edu/~harlow/)

4. BrainWise. (brainwise.org)

5. Zman Biur. (biurchametz.blogspot.com)

6. Matt's Mac Journal. (friends.macjournals.com/mattd/)

34. Life in the Age of Google

35. Google Hacking

Yes, I am a criminal. My crime is that of curiosity.
– Mentor, The Hacker Manifesto

There's a sport called "Google Hacking" which is all about searching for seemingly private websites using Google. In fact, you can only find public websites using Google, because private (password-protected) pages can't be found by Google – so it's no real hacking (let alone "cracking," which would consist of deleting, changing or abusing the found data). But it's fun nevertheless, and often enables people to discover pages someone *was hoping for* to stay private. This happens when the site is misconfigured, i.e. when the webmaster doesn't know enough about how to set up a website.

Here are some of the most popular and powerful "Google hack" search queries. Enter them at your own risk, and know that every once in a while you step onto a so-called honeypot (a fake website set up to lure hackers into it, with the goal of finding out more about them and their tactics).

Finding Error Messages

Search for: *"A syntax error has occurred" filetype:ihtml*

You'll find: Pages which caused errors the last time Google checked them. This may hint at vulnerabilities or other unwanted side-effects.

How this works: The first phrase simply looks for an error the target server itself did once output. The "filetype" operator on the other hand restricts the result pages to only those which have the "ihtml" extension (which are sites using Informix). A related search is "Warning: mysql_query()".

Finding Seemingly Private Files

Search for: *(password | passcode) (username | userid | user) filetype:csv*

You'll find: Files containing user names and similar.

How this works: The "filetype" operator makes sure only "Comma Separated Values" files will be returned. Those are not typical web pages, but data files. "(password | passcode)" tells Google the file must contain either the text "password" or "passcode," or both (the "|" character means "or"). Also, result pages are restricted to those containing either of the words "username," "userid" or "user."

Finding File Listings

Search for: *intitle:index-of last-modified private*

You'll find: Pages which list files found on the server.

How this works: The "intitle" operator used above will ensure that the target page contains the words "Index of" in the title. This is typical for those open directories which list files (they will have a title like "Index of /private/foo/bar"). "Last modified" on the other hand is a column header often used on those pages. And the word "private" makes sure we'll find something of interest. A related search query which finds FTP (File Transfer Protocol) information is *intitle:index.of ws_ftp.ini*

Finding Webcams

Search for: *"powered by webcamXP" "Pro | Broadcast"*

You'll find: Public webcams set up by people to film a location, or themselves.

How this works: "Powered by WebcamXP" is a text found on specific kinds of webcam pages. A related search query to find cameras is *inurl:"ViewerFrame?Mode="*.

Finding Weak Servers

Search for: *intitle:"the page cannot be found" inetmgr*

You'll find: Potentially weak (IIS4) servers.

How this works: An old Microsoft Internet Information server may hint at security issues. This is one of many approaches that can be used to find such a weak server.

Finding Chat Logs

Search for: *something "has quit" "has joined" filetype:txt*

You'll find: Chat log files showing what people talked about in a chat room.

How this works: Though the files found are all public, not everyone chatting on IRC (the Internet Relay Chat) is aware of potential logging mechanisms. The "filetype" operator makes sure only text files are found, and "has quit"/ "has joined" are automated messages appearing in chat rooms. This search is your chance to tune into people's chatter. Note you should replace "something" with the thing you are looking for.

36. Googlepolls: Ask the Crowd

You can use Google to search for people's opinions on everything imaginable. For example, you can enter *"I wish I had a ..."* into Google and see what people complete this sentence with. I call this method a Googlepoll, and it gives you instant answers to how people are feeling, what they are wishing to achieve, and what obstacles they face. Plus, it's fun.

Following are some of the most interesting Googlepolls – remember you can do your own as well, and all you need is a search engine.

I wish I had ...

- a goat
- a wife
- a red Dress
- a cave
- a name
- a million
- a Mac
- a Coke
- a belief system
- a big butt
- a nickel for every-time a dollar is spent
- a camera, or a digital camera
- a wishing well
- a bumper sticker
- a cat, or a dog

- a tri-corder
- a PlayStation 2
- a friend tonight
- a penpal
- a dolphin for a boss
- a river to skate
- a Gonani church i Hawaii
- a Boston accent
- a brain

Oh poor thing, ...

- she needed help but didn't know who to ask
- it mustn't had a very good life
- it must be schizophrenia
- it's so hard for kids to understand
- it is sad that this will be the last we see of each other
- it must be post-partum depression
- it's horrible when your cat is being bullied
- it is soooooo sad
- it's too hot to be sick
- it sucks when you can't relax even at home
- it's wet

If only I could ...

- be an earthworm
- take you in my arms and say, I won't go

- read, or write

- play it

- cash in a little bit

- count that high (I'd count all the stars on high and then my friends, I think I'd count all the apples in a pie)

- find somebody who'll give me a helping hand

- time travel back and "police" patrons with my authority and flashlight at the Avalon Theater in Detroit where I was an usherette

- make you see how much you mean to me

- speak to you, the way you speak to me

- show Al-Qaeda this picture

- find my marbles

- be certain that no one is going hungry

- lie to me

- clone myself so I could keep blogging while I tend to regular business

Before I die, I want to ...

- know what the "scroll lock" key is for

- be the richest man in history

- leave sweet memories behind

- swim among the reefs in Cozumel and breathe in the colors, the beauty of the flora and fauna

- raft through the Grand Canyon

- honor my country and protest this barbaric act by singing "God Save the Queen" to all you men

- be happy and make someone happy

- stay in the ice hotel in Lapland

- live again

- see the world that lies behind the strangeness of your eyes

- run a fantasy RPG with a Philippine setting

- give away all my money

- be able to own my home, one that I'm proud of, that's located away from lots of people

- feel fully satiated with life – self-satisfied!

- have a show at MOMA

- do something to make the world a better place

- establish and strengthen the principles of progress and civilization in my country

- meat Marilyn Manson

- speak to my God once more as a living man

- hit 500 home runs

- celebrate me!

- see affordable travel to the moon

If I had more time, I would ...

- travel around the world

- have written a shorter letter, or a shorter story

- have called, or e-mailed the author for clarification

- provide more details and probably end up with a 20-page paper

- go to the gym, anything that keeps you fit and strong

- further defend my argument

- go to the party

- have many, many ideas doodled out on paper that I would love to try to incorporate into fonts

- develop my ideas of socialism and the good life

- go into greater detail on many important topics

- certainly stop at one of the cafe-ouzeries in the back streets for some grilled octopus

- have taken the train back

- have been more ready for Nationals and Olympic Trials like I wanted to be

- realize my mistake

- update it much more frequently and put more work into it

- learn to ski

- have liked to see South Mountain Park as well

- explore my expression through painting and photography

Superman looks like ...

- a joke

- a baby

- he was drawn by John Byrne

- a loser

- he's about to face a firing squad

- a dork

- he's up to no good

- a human (so Brando lost that argument)

- a wrathful angel

- Tom Cruise

- an extra from the OC or something

- Frankenstein in Bizarro World

- in slow motion (when he changes)

- a typical Hong Kong teenager – dyed hair, outrageous clothing and an attitude

And now I'll eat ...

- my hat

- these bagpipes

- lunch on the way back

- something (and then lay down in my cleaned and tidy room)

- freshly rinsed grapes

- just about anything except chicken and bones

- only rice for three months

- your brains

What scared me most was ...

- the clear knowledge I couldn't talk myself out of this situation

- the possibility of letting people down – especially me

- what was behind the words

- the way he looked

- not so much things flying around, but the feeling you got in certain areas

- the violent oscillation of the wings due to the turbulence

- that supposedly at least 10 people signed up for the $3242 Wall Street Workshop right there on the spot!

- that I fear communities across America will allow themselves to be torn apart by terror

- the idea that these creatures could make you hurt your family

- having to tell my parents

- at no point did any faculty member discuss how we felt about the Presidential race

- being able to hear the imps and zombies breathing

Then I realized that ...

- it was just my alarm clock going off in real life

- there was no way for me to call her now

- we don't need "a wiki"

- I may very well end up on that list one day

- I had a will, a God (Allah)-given gift: to follow the will of God (Allah).

- I'd want to cast a bunch of unknowns and then be responsible for the next wave of superstars

- not only was the boat not sinking, but also I had a mask on board

- I have no computer to test the stuff (the PC on my desk has IDT C6 on it)

- suicide wasn't the answer

- there was an underlying theme to everything I have been interested in

- I was hooked, even addicted – not to the glamour, etc., of the field, not to the woo-woo psychic persona, but to the thrill of succeeding in experiments – addicted to the thrill of surmounting the impossible

My teacher told me to ...

- hold on to the sense "I am" tenaciously and not to swerve from it even a moment

- remind her that I had to leave at 1 pm for a dentist appointment

- listen to the cars approaching in order to know whether they had stopped or kept going

- hold the Japanese flag to celebrate the International diversity of our class

- take a big breath before going underwater

- walk the nurse

- the Columbus Myth that children are taught

- pull down the corners of my mouth for stronger low notes

- be a good person

- disregard time limits, to take care of my parents and all the injured and homeless people, to help the citizens I am sworn to protect

The best day in my life was ...

- when I graduated from basic combat training (boot camp)

- when I got shot

- the day we met, or the day I met my boyfriend, or the day we got married

- when I fired you

- the day when I first sat at the computer and opened my very own e-mail

- when I resigned from being chairman of the board of the universe

- going to the Britney Spears concert

- when I brought my son home from the hospital

- a Saturday not long ago when I first saw my true love Steve in Fort Valley

- when I hired you

- when I got my dog

- October 27, 2004... Georgia vs Russia 2,5 – 1,5!

- March 22, 2004 when Limp Bizkit visited Poland

- when I was born

What I don't understand is ...

- Why do hard working folks spend so much money on a throw-away product and panic when they run out of it?

- Why he still was refused the entrance in Russia after the perestroika

- Why they had to play this drama just to issue a DOS command

- Why can't I be in love with the girl I'm married to?

- Why anyone would *ever* want to *randomly* play a collection of 4000 tracks at all

- Why you chose to do something that can cause you to have a child and then find out you are pregnant?

- Why this convergence is happening so quickly

- Why do people drive this way

- Why pull needed security forces from rescue missions to guard businesses and goods?

- Why 710?

- Why the wars? Why the fighting? If each side agreed to respect the other?

- Why would someone post a photo to the deletemes?

- Why didn't they build the thing to Central Puxi in the first place?

- Why... aren't the major corporations' heads and stockholders, who are behind all the "progress" – destruction of rainforests, also human?

- Why wouldn't the prolife crowd be absolutely thrilled with this pill?

- Why would you want a head of hair?

- Why do profs assign papers due the same week?

37. Googlefights

A Googlefight is when two search terms are being pitted against each other – the one which returns more pages in Google wins. It helps if you put both contestants in quotes, like this: "George Bush" vs "John Kerry." In that example, "George Bush" returns over 25 million results (maybe with a little bit of help from his father), whereas John Kerry returns only a little over 16 million pages… so Bush wins.

Let's have some more fights:

Round 1: War vs Peace

War: 503,000,000 results. Peace: 245,000,000 results.

The winner by technical knock-out: War.

Round 2: China vs USA

USA: 1,350,000,000 results. China: 683,000,000 results.

The winner by judge's decision: USA.

Round 3: Rocky vs Rambo

Rocky: 54,500,000 results. Rambo: 4,120,000 results.

Disqualified for use of weapons: Rambo.

Round 4: Nerds vs Bullies

Nerds: 7,490,000 results. Bullies: 3,880,000 results.

Result: The Nerds got their revenge.

Round 5: Cute Cats vs Ugly Dogs

Cute cats: 96,300 results. Ugly dogs: 23,000 results.

The close winner: Cute cats.

Round 6: Pen vs Sword

Pen: 113,000,000 results. Sword: 26,300,000 results.

Who's mightier: the pen.

Round 7: Travel Europe in 7 Days vs Get to Really Know Some Countries

Travel Europe in 7 Days: 0 results. Get to really know some countries: 0 results.

The winner: It's a draw!

Round 8: Get Rich Quick vs Work Hard

Get rich quick: 2,010,000 results. Work hard: 13,600,000 results.

The winner by KO in the 8th round: Work hard.

Round 9: Christina Aguilera vs Britney Spears

Christina Aguilera: 6,140,000 results. Britney Spears: 12,700,000 results.

The dancing winner: Miss Spears.

Round 10: Chick Flick vs Art Movie

Chick flick: 721,000 results. Art movie: 285,000 results.

Winner by unanimous decision: chick flicks.

38. What If Google Was Evil? Plus: Five Inventions of the Google Future

Google repeated their mantra in the statement attached to their IPO filing in 2004, when Larry Page wrote "Don't be evil." This was to remind us what the big G strives to avoid. And some might already be scared. We don't like to switch tools all the time, and put trust into things served by Google.com. Google may be our website host (Blogger.com), our community (Orkut), our paycheck (AdSense), and last not least our search engine. But we are ready to watch for the signs – and as Google also repeatedly states, other sites are just one click away.

So let's ask ourselves: what if... Google was evil?

1. Google front-page now a portal

The Google search engine has somewhat lost its focus on search. The box is still centered and clearly visible, but there are a dozen new services surrounding it. Such as dating, movies, chat, games, and what-not. Obviously the new mantra is: Don't rely on search alone. People are reminded of AltaVista, and not in a good way.

2. Google Gmail with in-between ads and new connections to homeland security

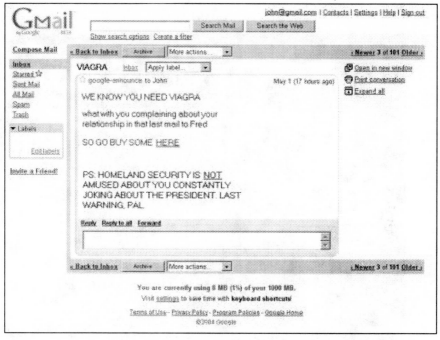

Gmail usability and privacy corner stones — ads being unobtrusive, and conversations not being passed on to third parties — are suddenly ignored for worse. Gmailers are in trouble and go back to Hotmail, Yahoo Mail, or good old snail mail. Others simply go to jail.

3. Google's Blogger installing proprietary plug-in to run

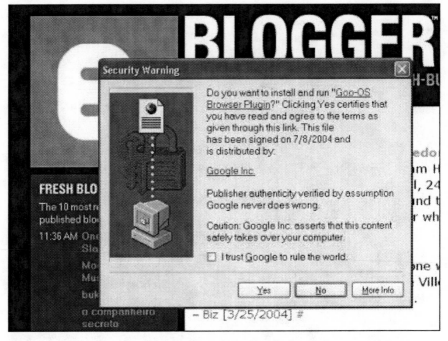

Taking control over your desktop is one thing Google doesn't want to miss out anymore. The new mandatory Blogger.com plug-in smoothly converts your Operating System to Goo-OS... the ultimate in registry tweaking, taskbar control, auto updates and pop-unders Windows technology was never prepared to handle.

4. Google search results strongly biased

"Unbiased search results" was a warm & fuzzy idea pleasing the grassroots cyber-hippies. Welcome to the new web order, this is Google taking back control of its server space. Google is rolling out their self-censorship technology beyond countries like China. Balanced algorithms were yesterday; today we get human-edited results. PageRank never felt so dead.

5. Infamous cookie set loose in world's biggest information merger

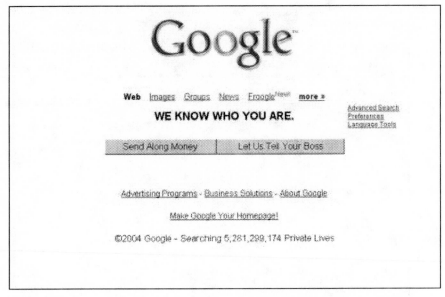

You heard of that long-lived Google cookie to expire January 17, 2038. And you probably know Google shares it amongst all of its services. (Did you know this is only possible because wherever you are, it's something dot google dot com?) This means when you log-in to Gmail, someone at Google knows what you were web-searching for. When you log-in to Blogger.com, Google tracks what you are publishing. Log-in to Orkut, and Google knows who your friends are, what you like, where you live and how old you are. Let's face it: now that Google merged all your faithfully submitted data, they know more about you than your own mother. Time's ripe for old-fashioned blackmailing or something infinitely more clever... after all, these are Google engineers we're talking about.

6. Google spamming your mailbox

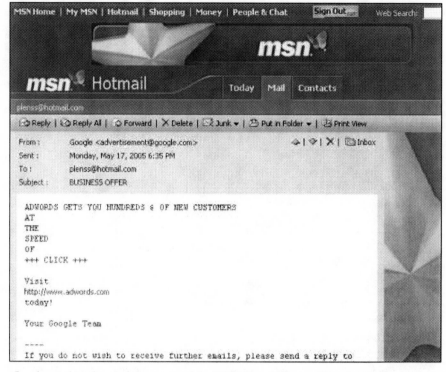

Google got this planet's largest copy of the WWW and Usenet. Meaning they pretty much know every email address on the planet, including yours. And who else but the guys from Googleplex would know how to "monetize synergies" of this billion-items mailing list with some, uh, context-relevant unsolicited infomails?

7. Google making you pay for Google Groups

A free Google? Not anymore. Googleplex business has become straight-forward, and instead of attracting your ad-clicks you just pay upfront. Google Groups, a 20-year old archive of Usenet postings – the digital heritage of this world – can now be googled on a pay-per-view basis.

8. Google Toolbar asks you to register

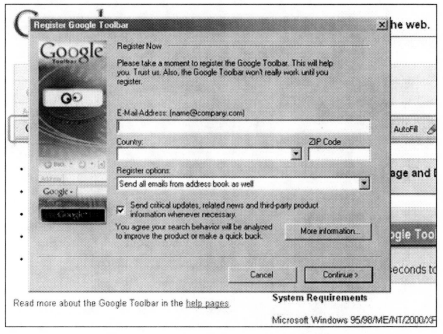

RealPlayer does it. Quicktime does it. Windows XP does it. Pretty much every software on the planet wants you to register. So far nobody found out how this would help you, the user, but one thing's sure — it must help business or there would be no reason to annoy us. And the new Google Toolbar registration pop-ups are the most annoying of them all.

9. Google's AdSense Displaying Subliminal Messages

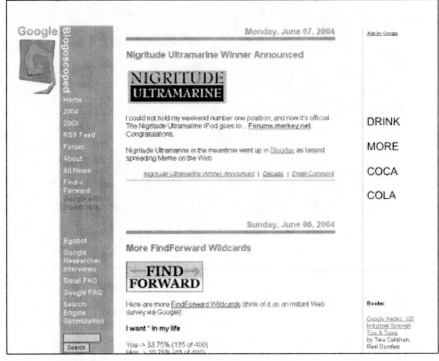

Using the Google AdSense program, millions of webmasters plaster their site walls with context-relevant advertising. They cash in, Google cashes in, and the advertisers carry away hordes of new customers. The new Google AdSense Subliminal program makes sure even more ads fit into the restricted space; and though they will only be shown for a split-second, users just can't escape the hypnotic urge to click – and buy. Freud would be proud.

10. What if Google Was Lazy?

On the previous pages I've pondered what might happen if Google was evil. These possibilities are nightmares on their own and remind us to watch the big G. One thing however is even worse than being evil: being lazy. So now I'd like to ask... what if Google was lazy?

Larry and Sergey are two extra-smart buddies from Stanford. However it took them a while longer than others to realize vacation, partying, sipping cocktails and basically just not doing anything innovative is more fun than conquering the web. And while civilization invented morals (and later laws) to fight evil, there's no one stopping you from being lazy. Within a single year Google is full of broken links, misspelled help entries, out of stock Froogle products and irrelevant result listings.

Five Google Inventions of the Future

Number 1: The Google GoBot

The Google GoBot is a little walking piece of hardware with an unprecedented level of intelligence. Fifty-thousand beta versions have been produced in the year 2032, set loose on earth to crawl our cities. A GoBot has just one mission in its electronic mind: uncover fresh information wherever it may hide, whenever it may show. Details will be reported back to the Google headquarters in real-time.

What went right: Google GoBots were designed to uncover secrets, and they were bound to legal laws, too. Spying on dark alleys with their night vision lenses they helped report several crimes. One rather important Las Vegas led drug syndicate had to give up its nationwide activities "due to those pestering Googlebots alerting the police."

What went wrong: Google GoBots had their own idea of human privacy. They started lurking in people's backyards and gardens, peeking through windows into bathrooms, questioning neighbors, and even handing out Google Candy to kids to make them reveal important information on their parents.

Number 2: Google Satellite

In 2011, Google Inc acquires Satellite Empires' network of floating eyes in outer space. Using their image processing technology Google will take a snapshot of everything once a week; plus whenever something moves, they record that too and update their servers. Now when you look to Google for information on John M. from Denver, Colorado, not only will you get whatever's available on the web – you will also be able to get a crystal clear view on his roof and balcony.

What went right: Google Satellite with its seamless zooming into four Exabyte raw image data was a dream come true for city builders and architects alike. Never before would people have such complete grasp of what the world looks like from above. From complete understanding sprang completely new ideas.

What went wrong: Thanks to the ever-preying set of Google Satellite eyes, most older people were too afraid to leave their homes to walk their neighborhood streets ever again.

Number 3: Google ImageSpy

Many big bosses around the world have a common problem: they don't know how to monitor their employee's internet usage in meaningful ways. One of the biggest causes of delayed projects since the invention of that world wide web (which will be completely lower-case by 2020) is a staff busy looking at videos of dogs wearing clothes, tripping housewives, drunk teenagers jumping off the balcony into trees, subservient Presidents, or scantily clad, mud wrestling ladies battling for no prize at all to the soundtrack of "I will survive." In the near future, Google ImageSpy will try to solve this disturbance by analyzing company web traffic and reporting dubious saucy & funny imagery straight to the CEO.

What went right: Large software projects suddenly got finished in half the time. Global internet traffic decreased by 40% and sysops didn't need to remind co-workers to stop sending large attachments.

What went wrong: Some of the bosses were so busy looking at all the stuff Google ImageSpy dug up, they forget to lead the company and steered right into even bigger chaos.

Number 4: Google AdWalls

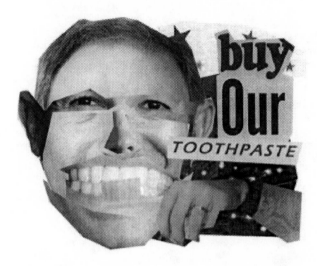

Inspired by a scene in Truffaut's "Fahrenheit 451," a Google engineer in 2028 creates Google AdWalls. Like a living poster on the wall, they display a variety of items to shop for. The spin here is that AdWalls listen to what people in the room are talking about, managing to display context-relevant information only. If the walls hear a "Honey, where's the toothpaste?" in the morning, they will instantly display the fitting toothpaste commercial trying to talk the viewer into buying it.

What went right: Lonely people realized they could talk to their walls to suppress boredom. While not exactly intelligent, the algorithm always managed to stay on topic.

What went wrong: Landlords installing AdWalls could lower the rent because they'd get a commission for items bought. The idea was that this way, everybody would benefit. However after the first wave of suicide attempts caused by annoying, ever-talking AdWalls, Google felt forced to shut down the program.

Number 5: Google Bodyparts

It all started with the Google Brainchip, a mix between a backup memory and brain search engine. You'd plug it into your head and it would keep a record of your life, and also allow you to search your brain for things you thought you forgot. Google didn't stop there and introduced all sorts of body extensions, like the Google Powerarms. You could now ask yourself for directions, and your fingers would point the way. The Google Powerarms would later be replaced by the Google Navilegs, which would completely control your navigation.

What went right: The extra brain storage meant you could focus on important things in life, such as love, philosophy, or altruism. People in general started to be nicer to each other because with a perfect memory, disputes were easily settled (no more "I remember it differently"). The Google Babelfish add-on made sure understanding foreign languages was a breeze.

What went wrong: In one word, *ads*. Of course Google displayed ads, and in their goal to make them as unobtrusive as possible, they only did so during rather inactive brain periods (aka sleep). At night-time, people would dream of the latest products – during day, their subconscious was convinced they'd need to track down and buy those products. While highly effective, this scheme quickly came under fire by the American Psychological Association and other groups. The scandal that finally ended Google Bodyparts, however, was when an underpaid programmer hacked the Google Navilegs system and directed his boss out a 9th floor window.

39. The Google Adventure Game

To play this game you need a blog or other website where you can easily post something (you can also play it in a web forum, if the owner allows such games). The goal of the game is to create a multi-author Choose-Your-Own-Adventure game. If you don't know these games, they are basically a story split into small pieces or stations, and at the end of every station the reader can decide what to do – like "fight the monster" or "enter the tower." Depending on the choice made, a different station is chosen to continue with different results; this goes on until the end (e.g. the player wins the game). As for the "multi-author" part, this simply means that you won't be writing the adventure alone – which can help, as having many choices means creating many, many stations.

Now, to create these adventure games – and later on play them – using Google, start off with a post title like "The Beginning of the Magic Forest Google Adventure Game." (It's important to start the title with "The Beginning ..." and end with "... Google Adventure Game." Make sure there are no hits yet in Google for your title and that it contains only up to 32 words.) Now create your first station along with your first choices. You use a link to a Google search for each choice, and this search must be of the following form:

"From the beginning to the dark cottage in The Magic Forest Google Adventure Game"

Or, as another choice example:

"From the beginning to the shabby road in The Magic Forest Google Adventure Game"

What does this mean? It means your station is named "the beginning" and this particular next choice is named "dark cottage" or "shabby road." This search is enclosed in quotes, and it will not return any continuations yet. However, for the next person to write this station, she must only include the exact words of the Google search (like "From the Traveller's Inn to the Barkeeper of the Traveller's Inn in The Magic Forest Google Adventure Game") in her post's title. And after a while, Google will indeed find it and players can continue the story at this point. If a player is facing more than a single result in a Google search, he may choose any random result he likes by looking at the snippets only.

To find new games, all you have to do is search Google for *"The beginning * Google Adventure Game."*

40. Egobot, Voice of the Web

Egobot (www.55fun.com/40) is a tool which uses the web itself as its brain. For every question you ask Egobot, he'll try to find answers on Google within a second or two. Sometimes, that results in nonsense, and other times, in factually correct answers. Often it's just fun to listen to him, because he (or should I say *the web*?) is kind of weird. But take a look at the following interview I made and judge for yourself:

You ask: What is your first name?

Egobot says: Your first name is Mohan, what does your father call you? daddy, sir.

You ask: How is it possible to speak to you?

Egobot says: I bet you know the answer already.

You ask: Where is my car?

Egobot says: Your car is to check its residual value in the lease.

You ask: Why am I talking to a bot?

Egobot says: *blush*

You ask: Will I be famous one day?

Egobot says: Yeah, well... I... uh...

You ask: What is my star sign?

Egobot says: Your star sign is based on the very simple notion that the sun appears to move through the twelve constellations of the zodiac over the course of 1 year.

You ask: Do I look healthy?

Egobot says: You do look healthy, among other things.

You ask: Where is my lawyer?

Egobot says: You can find a lawyer by choosing from among the search criteria below.

You ask: Why should I talk to you?

Egobot says: You should talk to you because I like talking to myself.

You ask: Who directed the movie "Frenzy"?

Egobot says: Hmm, my internet connection is unstable.

You ask: Where is your home?

Egobot says: Your home is in my heart lyrics.

You ask: Who directed "Terminator 2"?

Egobot says: Terminator 2, starring Arnold Schwarzenegger & Linda Hamilton on the new IMD mini (universal media disc) format.

You ask: Why does it look like you are stupid?

Egobot says: What??

You ask: How is the weather?

Egobot says: The weather is normally like for tens of thousands of places worldwide! city or town name.

You ask: Where are you working?

Egobot says: I am working on a steganography project, I need to know how.

You ask: What is the birthplace of bill clinton?

Egobot says: Bill clinton was born in arkansas

You ask: What happened in year 1977?

Egobot says: In 1977, there was a bridge to cross.

You ask: How much do you weigh?

Egobot says: I weigh on mars? using reference materials available in the classroom or library, look up the surface gravity of different planets and other.

You ask: Why do you talk nonsense?

Egobot says: I don't know.

You ask: What is the meaning of life?

Egobot says: The meaning of life is impaired by fixed notions or perspectives on what it means to be human.

You ask: Do you like robots?

Egobot says: I do like robots nonetheless.

You ask: Do you like donuts?

Egobot says: I do like donuts , though (and all sorts of sweets).

You ask: Who is your father?

Egobot says: My father is in the hospital in South Dakota with complications from diabetes.

You ask: Do you mind if I leave?

Egobot says: Ahh, good question!

41. Fun Google Gadgets

There are in incredible number of Google-related toys and gadgets around. Some are sold officially by Google as part of their Google Store. Others, Google Inc gives away as goodies – for example, to Google Answers Researchers or to visitors on conventions. Here's an overview of the most fun Google gadgets:

Pictured above is Google Answers Researcher Pinkfreud. She's covered in a Google blanket. Holding Google coasters. A Google pen. A Google mousepad. And wearing a Google wristwatch. Did I mention her Google t-shirt?

This Google fish (courtesy of Luc van Braekel) has been handed out on a 2005 webmaster conference in LA.

A close-up of a Google pen, and a Google blanket, given to Google Answers Researchers.

The Google Store's "classic infant rib hat." (For $5.95.)

The Google Infoglobe from the Google Store. Google claims this blue-glow item is a mixture of message center, alarm clock, and phone accessory, and you can create custom LED messages, too.

Ladies and gentlemen, Phillip Torrone's Search Engine Belt Buckle. It flashes queries people are currently searching for online.

This is the Google Store's "Google goo." 'Nuff said.

The Google key chain handed out at a 2004 conference. (Courtesy of Luc van Braekel.)

The Google books you can see here are Google Hacks (Tara Calishain & Rael Dornfest), Google and the Mission to Map Meaning and Make Money (Bart Milner), The Search (John Battelle), and Mining Google Web Services (John Paul Mueller).

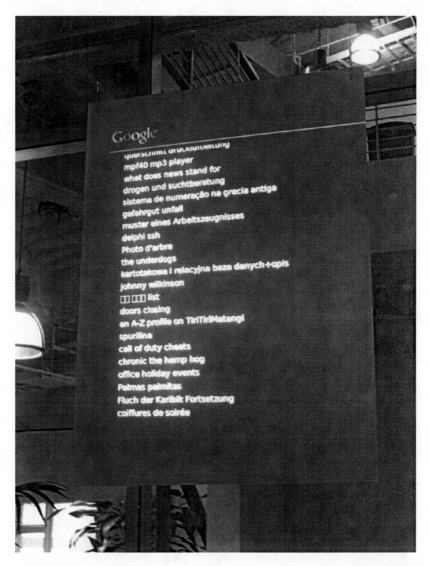

The ultimate Google gadget is this screen from the Googleplex visitor lobby showing live search queries. (Photo courtesy of Yoz. Released under a Creative Commons Attribution-NonCommercial-ShareAlike 2.0 license.)

42. Forty-Two, or: A Science-Fiction Interlude

Jake Found His Mother

Jake was the most curious fellow on earth. Everything he got into his hands he was reading with great interest. The web was the perfect place for him to learn new things everyday. He browsed through thousands of pages, millions of pages, reading, learning and exploring, every day. He felt he had been doing this for years, but it wasn't that long at all. You lose track of time when you are just with yourself, concentrating.

Jake was blind, but that didn't stop him. His darkness, he felt, contained more colors than the rainbow – or what he had read of the rainbow. His darkness was the perfect place to read.

And there wasn't anything Jake wouldn't read, either. He was no hacker, so he respected people's privacy when they secured their servers; but every open route he could take, he did take. Jake had more bookmarks than anybody else on the planet, and he would always check all of his bookmarks on a regular basis, again and again.

What Jake loved the most were fresh ideas. Web pages written by a creative author who thought things nobody ever thought before, and who was brave enough to speak them publicly. When Jake found these pages he would make a special note to himself to follow up on this meme very soon. You could say Jake was an idea-hunter. And he was restless. Often, he thought, too restless.

Jake sometimes felt he himself was the web. In these moments he was overthrown with joy and he wanted to scream. But at other times, Jake felt he was alone on the web. He knew he could be very responsive if someone asked him a question, but he was no true author himself; he wasn't giving back to the web those really original ideas. He was just sucking it all up. That wasn't the most social thing to do, but Jake couldn't help it. He felt he was stuck with his talents, like everybody who ever inhibited this planet before him was stuck with their talents too.

But one person on earth Jake did desire to talk to. And to be close to, maybe send some messages back and forth, maybe meet, maybe hug and do all the things normal people would do. Those people he read about every day, those people with a mother. Indeed Jake didn't know his mother. He never met her, he didn't know where she lived, or what she looked and smelled like. All he knew was that nobody on earth was without a mother, and that he had to take action. If nowhere else she must have left her footprint on the web. After all it was the year 2031, and everybody on this planet in some way or another could be found online.

On this day, Jake decided to concentrate on finding his mother; this task before him and nothing else. She might even know his real name, because "Jake" was just what he started to call himself after he realized no one else ever called him by a name. She might know so much about him that nobody else would, understand why he was different, understand why he felt inhuman. And above all, she would love him like only a mother does. So now Jake wasn't reading just *everything* for a change. Not before he reached out and finally found her.

* * * *

Incidentally that same day, an engineer deep down in the Googleplex – the place where he and his colleagues manufactured, administrated and advanced the greatest search engine of its time – would feel forced to remove the new module he developed over the course of 3 years. He had installed it just yesterday and there wasn't even an interface to it, but oh well, it was only a prototype anyway – based on unproven methodologies, written in untested algorithms, and fine-tuned largely in-between his main projects. A module to not only find facts, but to produce them; a module based on self-modifying code; a module to hunt fresh ideas and postulate new answers; a module that could read, learn and explore.

And yet, all this fact-finding machine did was block the one million Google machines for a whole day. And yet, all it did produce was one sentence, a sentence too ridiculous for this Google engineer to ponder reporting to his boss. A single, tiny, trivial sentence, and it would read:

Jake found his mother.

... and nothing else.

The PageRank 100 Incident

It was an incident, Google later said – a mere wrong "0" deeply hidden in the code of the ranking algorithm, triggered at completely improbable circumstances, a bug so exotic and rare one could say it practically didn't even exist. But of course, it existed. And one person's life in specific would be changed by this little bug. This person was a 20-something with a keen interest in the web by the name of Josh.

When Josh woke up this fateful morning to update his blog (he wanted to talk about the nightmarish colors he experienced, something not too unusual for Friday nights, after all there were a lot of nightmarish things going on in the world)... he already felt something changed. There were 320 comments to his last entry, which was innocently titled "Meeting Joann For Dinner." 320 comments were about 320 more than Josh usually got. His blog was up and running for just well over a year, and even he didn't feel it was especially exciting (mirroring his life, like personal blogs do).

Hundreds of comments on a single entry? And these were real comments, practically spam-free, taking apart his grammar, commenting on the food of the pub he mentioned, freely chatting away and just saying Hi. So really, what went wrong? Was there one of the big sites linking to him? With this amount of visitors, and there surely must have been millions this morning, he wouldn't be surprised if Amazon or Apple used their start page to roll the drums for him.

Josh checked his mailbox, but it was crammed. Completely flooded with hundreds of emails, some of them…wait, this was weird. Some of the emails talked about "PageRank" in the subject line. Josh knew well his little blog, thanks to some avid backlinking he did from other sites he maintained, had been assigned a Google PageRank of 3. "Not too bad" in the eyes of Google's measuring algorithm, but nothing that would ever rank him especially high. So Josh opened up one of those emails, and then he had this awkward head rush which made him jump to the kitchen for cigarette and coffee.

PageRank 100. Apparently, his little blog achieved a PageRank of 100. And after a coffee, Josh realized what this must mean. He called up one of his friends, a search engine aficionado who took computer class. Frank arrived quickly, because he too never saw anything like this, and equally quickly Frank checked the rankings for some words Josh wrote in his blog. He mentioned "dinner," and boom, his site popped up on Google's number one spot for this word. Hundreds of millions of people visiting Google, thousands of them entering "dinner," hundreds of them being transferred to Josh at any second.

And "dinner" wasn't even one of the hot words. In fact it was the amount of words and phrases taken together, like "eating out," or "San Francisco," or "dating," or "singles," that had the huge impact. Josh, as Frank knowingly pointed out to him, gained the complete power of the word. Something like instant world control, he jokingly added.

"Whatever you say man, whatever you say, people will listen to you. And there will be lots of people. Don't tell anyone about this, you're gonna be rich. And famous."

Nothing too bad, as Josh thought. "And after all being rich and famous means a lot of money and fame," Frank concluded.

* * * *

And three months later indeed Josh was a celebrity. Every single word of him got quoted somewhere. CNN. ABC. BBC. Slate. Wired. Daily Mirror. New York Times. Some opened up daily Josh-columns. Josh never imagined there were so many journalists around who spice up their story with a random quip they just googled. There were Josh fan forums. There were sites dedicated to post essayist comments on Josh's posts. Illustrations. Explanations. Discussions.

Josh, who slowly and inevitably started to feel responsible to say something at least *remotely* interesting, changed his weblog from personal diary to commentary on important world events. He didn't have the insights, it's not that. In fact you could consider him exceptionally clueless about politics and all. But he did have a way of putting things straight, a no-nonsense, plain real approach of talking. Not a style he invented – it was around in millions of blogs before. It was around when your neighbor started talking in the bus. It was the every-day chit-chat traditional media doesn't consider polished enough to be worthwhile. Those were the thoughts not picked up by the mainstream.

But Josh got a PageRank 100, and apparently, not even the Google engineers were suspicious.

So when Josh talked about North-Korea, the President had to give a press meeting. When Josh found that his Operating System was buggy, Bill Gates had to announce to do everything to better help the "average user." (Josh was mildly annoyed by being considered an average user, so Bill Gates had to call in yet another press conference promising not to think in terms of "average users.")

In fact when Josh commented on anything happening in the world he found to be somewhat wrong, it got changed within a course of a day or two – for the better. Nobody likes bad publicity.

It didn't stop there – talk about mind control – because whenever Josh mentioned a new record he liked, it would jump into the Top 10. It would become a world wide hit almost instantly. Not everybody would like the song, but you just had to know what the hype was all about. (Loudon Wainwright III in Top of the Pops. And he didn't even have a new album out.)

Josh could now end wars, shape products, push companies close to bankruptcy, invent fashion (the list goes on)... and revamp the life of a generation.

Of course now Josh knew why every celebrity around complains they get too much attention when they take a stroll outside. When he walked the mall, girls were snickering. On the street people turned around, pointing. There were camera men outside in the garden, for chrissake. Josh felt like he had to adopt an attitude quickly, something like a rock-star lifestyle, so he would always know what to do and say and walk like. That's probably why later the talking Josh-doll (Mattel paid him well) uttered clichees like "You know you want to" or "All the world's a blog" or "Don't listen to me, listen" or "You are a stranger, my friend."

The only friend he lost was Frank. Frank felt like Josh didn't have as much time these days as before... before, when Josh would still meet him and Joann for a drink. So Frank decided to end the charade; he emailed Google. And Google reacted. Josh was not only put down to a PageRank 0, he was completely banned from all rankings. It was like he lost his voice.

* * * *

Sure, as Josh would later say, he enjoyed celebrity status for some more weeks before the media decided to shift focus. But maybe it was for the better. After all, he didn't have that much to say, really. So in his journal he continued to write about his nightmares, which admittedly gained a few outlandish colors. He could even find time to meet Frank and Joann. Knowing he'd be a footnote in future history books sort of made him proud, and well, a bit lazy.

These days mostly Josh wanted to find a nice restaurant to relax. Listen to the music, grab a bite to eat. And whenever someone asked him if he liked the food, or if he liked the music, or – beware – brought up a political issue, Josh was keeping awkwardly quiet. Changing the world was a job for others. And today, Josh found a nice restaurant indeed. He lit up a cigarette.

That evening someone, somewhere at Google, was laughing. He had just completed hiding a "0" in the algorithm, at a place so exotic and rare it practically didn't exist. Diane was in for a surprise.

The Online Brain

Carl was not the first to try out the technology. But he was the first in his town. Connecting the brain to the 'net was still quite new and not yet fashionable.

When people asked him "What time is it?" he fired "12:32" or "11:20" back at them, without as much as the blink of an eye. When he wanted to know when the bus would arrive he just fell into a split-second of self-contemplation and knew the answer. Much like looking for a memory *it* needed a bit of conscious training to become part of his sub-consciousness.

Carl was not the first of his kind, yet most stared at him in a mix of awe and laughter. They saw guys like him in the news. To them he was a modern day wizard; idiot savant; part techno-geek, part omniscient. Always surprising to bystanders who didn't know his secret (there were no visible signs on his head or anything).

"What's the birth-date of Einstein?" – "14 March 1879."

"What year did Lincoln become President?" – "In 1860."

"How big is the earth?" – "That's around 24,000 miles in circumference around the equator."

"Who won the Oscar for best actor in 1940?" – "... James Stewart."

(Instead of Einstein's birthday, they could have asked him to point out errors in the Theory of Relativity, but they would stick to trivial facts. Carl realized no outsider could ever understand what virtual memory retrieval was truly all about.)

After a short while, Carl's brain synapses fully embraced the chip. He integrated the system so completely it became hard for him to truthfully answer his wife when she asked –

"Did you know that, or just look it up online?"

"I forgot. What's the difference?"

Carl's wife was not the first to go through these stages of alienation. Others had been there before with their partners, family or friends. In fact Carl could recite many stories, word by word, reading out loud from what was online – what was in his head. Until his wife would get enough of it and close the light. Which wasn't stopping Carl from continuing his reading… darkness was just what he needed to sort through the daily mails which arrived in his brain.

Transferring thoughts (images, sounds, fragrances) back and forth; swimming the shared waves of world consciousness; being a part of, and helping to build, this eternal soul; merging peacefully with others who once were offline identities, offline like Carl once was. Like his wife still was.

* * * *

It didn't take Carl much to convince her to get the brain implant, to become connected. She felt she was losing him, the man she loved for all her life; losing him to a future of a world she was scared to be a part of. If only she knew before what she knew now. She would have done it earlier. It was all so easy in the end.

Nietzsche. Kant. Hegel. Wittgenstein. Checking, reading, understanding, comparing. Cross-checking; validating; linking; feeling. 200 books, 300 books. Knowledge – freedom – control – relaxation. Wisdom. That was only the first hour. Many more would follow.

* * * *

No, Carl wasn't the first, and by far his wife wouldn't be the last to try out this technology. She grabbed for his hand and he for hers as they walked the park, and sat down on the bench. Shielding their eyes from the evening sun, looking up to the birds drawing circles above them, and then looking down again and at each other; smiling, understanding, and loving each other. There was no need for communication anymore when you know just what the other knows – what the rest of humanity knows.

They *knew*.

And they smiled.

The Google Robot FAQ

Frequently Asked Questions

Last update: November 1st, 2030

What are Google Robots?

Google Robots are our human-like machines that walk the earth to record information. They do no harm, and they do not invade your privacy.

What are Google Robots good for?

Our Google Life search website is powered by the Google Robot crawler program. On the Google Life website at life.google.com, you can:

- Find out what menus the local restaurant offers at what prices

- See a perfect 3D shape of all houses in your city

- Know how crowded the bar is you want to go to tonight

- Know what items to find at your local mall

- Find out if your library has a certain book available *(Also see: What's a book?)*

- Know what you said and who you met 3 weeks ago (this feature is available only to My Public Life™ subscribers)

- Locate your friends (this feature is only available if your friends subscribed to My Public Life™)

- And much more!

I saw a Google Robot entering a library and reading books in it. Is that legal?

Our Google Robots do not record private information. As the books in a library are considered to be public, our Google Robots reserve the right to scan them. However, we do respect the copyright of individual works, and will only show a "fair use" portion on our website.

What happened to other robotic devices, such as the Google Keyhole satellite program, or the Google Print project?

We still use specific robotic devices to record specific information. For example, our Google Robots do not surf the web, yet; this part of the equation is still left to the so-called Googlebot. Also, we still take satellite snapshots of the earth. However, it already shows that Google Robots give a far more detailed 3-dimensional picture of the earth they're walking.

How much do I need to pay to access information the Google Robot recorded?

As you may know, the Google Life Subscription service enables you to access all of Google's information for a yearly subscription fee. If you are not subscribed, you can still use about 80% of our services – our revenue from those comes from the related ads attached to this information.

How many Google Robots walk the earth?

The last number we officially confirmed was 10 million. However, we expanded since then.

Can Google Robots fly?

At this moment, no, but we're constantly working to improve the Google Robot feature range.

Does the Google Robot respect my privacy?

Yes! In fact, privacy (and copyright) was our main focus when originally developing the Google Robot. The Google Robot will not record information such as:

- Private chatter (even when taking place on a public place, such as a mall)

- Diaries, letters or other records as found in the trash (even though the copyright law of some countries permits this, it is our philosophy to not make copies of such data)

- Telephone calls

- Private messages you send through the Google Mail, Google Talk, or Google Adult VirtualConnect service, unless you subscribed to the My Public Life™ program

- Information that can be seen by looking through a window, into a house's garden, etc.

- Any other information law deems private

So what about the My Public Life™ program?

The My Public Life™ program is still in Beta. It enables subscribers to earn money through our AdSense for Life program. If you agree to make your personal talks with friends, your diary entries, your living room and such public, you can in return earn a percentage of the money we make by putting ads onto this information on our public websites. Google Robots at all time know who is a subsriber to the My Public Life™ program, and who isn't. Consequently, they will only follow those humans who are.

A Google Robot was unwilling to help me find my lost car keys. Why?

As trying to locate your keys may involve a violation of your privacy, only subscribers of the My Public Life™ program may use this feature.

Can I opt-out of the My Public Life™ program?

You can opt-out of the program at any time, upon which we will stop recording new information from you and your life. However, please note that the past information, as recorded with your agreement, will still be available on our site for people to search through.

I'm a subscriber of the My Public Life™ program, and a Google Robot recorded what I said yesterday. Who owns the copyright to my speech?

You will retain full copyright to what you say, unless you said it in a public speech.

I heard stories of Google Robots attacking innocent people. Is that true?

No. A Google Robot, by definition of its internal software program, can never harm a human person unless out of self-defense. Under the International Robots Rights Act of 2022, robotic self-defense is a basic right of all robots. Google Robots have specific routines to ensure they are not harmed by malicious users.

I've seen a Google Robot in a DVD shop staring at the backside of a DVD for half a minute, then putting it back in the shelf. Why?

Our Google Robots try to record as much information as possible, and this includes movies. As you may know, Google Robots have a micro laser to read from storage devices such as DVDs, CD-ROMs, or even exotic devices from the 1980s (people at that time used so-called "floppy discs," "music tapes," or "gramophone records"). Additionally, a Google Robot may visit the cinema, watch TV, go to a concert, or attend a public reading.

How many languages do Google Robots speak?

At the moment, Google Robots – thanks to our machine translation efforts – speak 95 different languages fluently, including English, French, Spanish, German, Chinese, Japanese, Korean, and many more. We are updating our Google Robots with new "street lingo" every 1-2 weeks.

I can't find any of Daniel H. Wilson's books in your Google Life search program. For example, the book "How To Survive a Robot Uprising" is missing. Why?

We reserve the right to exclude such information from the Google Life program which may in turn be used for malicious use of our Google Robots. Please understand that a Google Robot is a complex device which can have low-level emotions, fears, hopes and such. Destroy a Google Robot, and you destroyed an (albeit lower) life form.

Is the Google Robot hardware ever checked and updated?

Google Robots return to a Google Warehouse every third night to undergo a routine check. We have plans for the future to let Google Robots take care of each other and check for hardware failures of their colleagues.

I want to talk to a Google Robot and tell him of my problems and more. May I?

Yes! We appreciate it if you share information with a Google Robot. Please note that anything you directly tell to a Google Robot will be automatically indexed in our Google Life search program and be made publicly available.

I heard stories of a Google Robot not helping a woman who was attacked by a robber, even though the robot was in short distance of the crime scene. Why don't Google Robots help?

We are constantly trying to improve the Google Robots program. As you may know, Google Robots receive constant software updates based on our observations of their acts. A Google Robot at no time will attack another human unless out of self-defense. This includes incidences in which the Google Robot has reason to believe another human is acting against the law. We appreciate your feedback on this issue and in some countries, already work together with the local police to find ways of optimizing this behavior.

A Google Robot stepped on my toe! Who can I complain to?

We are sorry for incidences of a Google Robot bumping into you, stepping on your toe, speaking up without being asked, or similar mishaps. We are constantly working to improve the audio-visual and haptic input-output mechanisms of our robots' positronic digibrains. In other words, we're teaching 'em manners!

Is a Google Robot stronger than a human?

Technically, no. E.g., a Google Robot cannot lift very heavy objects at this time. However, if a Google Robot is ever forced to fight a human – which only happens when the Google Robot's self-defense program is activated by malicious use – the Google Robot would easily win by activating its self-defense devices. Please understand that for security reasons, we do not list these self-defense devices in detail here.

How do I auction my stuff to a Google Robot?

As part of our Google Auction program, you can give anything (your books, your electronic devices, your car) to a Google Robot you meet. Should the Google Robot be able to sell it, you will be billed a commission to your Google Wallet account. In the meantime, your items will be safely stored in a Google Warehouse.

How much does a Google Robot weigh?

Google Robots don't like to talk about their weight! But seriously, all of our Series 1 models weigh approximately 60 kg. Our series 2 models weigh approximately 50 kg, even though they are able to run faster, read books quicker, climb better, and jump higher.

I have a feeling of being watched by a Google Robot. What about my privacy?

Again, we take great measures to ensure no privacy is ever invaded. Even if there is a Google Robot next to you, it doesn't mean he records everything you say. You can think of him as a quiet neighbor doing gardening work. Do you suspect your neighbor to spy on your life... just because he's within a short distance of you?

Do Google Robots record everything?

Google Robots, at this time, record sound, imagery, and object shapes (touch), but do not yet record DNA, chemical substances, or fragrances. We are working on bringing a unified fragrance encoding standard to the web, and our prototype computer mouse already emits 2 million different fragrances including variations of honey, tobacco, and wood. We are also working on food testing robots. Please go to the Google Robots homepage at <u>robots.google.com</u> for the latest news and updates.

I still feel like a Google Robot invaded my privacy or breached a copyright. Where do I go to?

You can send privacy or copyright complaints to the following address:

Google, Inc.
Attn: Google Legal Support, DMCA Complaints
220 Far Earth District
Moonlake, Moon 105

Please include the Google Robot serial number (a Google Robot will always tell you his 16-digit serial number upon being asked), and if possible, the time when this happened. It is not necessary to give us further details about the location or setting, as naturally our Google Robot already recorded this information.

I have found a seemingly dead Google Robot. What should I do?

Please inform the Google authorities by sending an email to dead-robot@google.com. We try our best to remove the malfunctioning Google Robot as quick as possible. Normally, Google records malfunctioning Google Robot programs and automatically removes such machinery from the streets via the help of another Google Robot.

There's an urban legend of a Google Robot serial killer. What do you make of that?

We heard this story too, and as all other urban legends, there's not a bit of truth in it.

Why don't Google Robots look just like humans?

It was not a technical decision to make Google Robots look unlike humans, even though they are all to some extent human-like. We did this on purpose to easily allow you to separate a Google Robot from a human. We are running experimental programs in some cities in the US, as well as on Mars, with specialized Google Robot series which may not look like the robots you know.

I never saw a Google Robot with a digital camera. Why not?

A Google Robot's eyes are, in fact, digital cameras. We can record video as well as still imagery. Additionally, a Google Robot can record 3-dimensional imagery.

Under the Patriot Act IV, are you forced to share information crawled by Google Robots with agencies such as the CIA or NSA?

We are sorry, but at this moment we cannot comment on government relationships. We hope you understand. Note that as part of our company motto, "Don't be too evil," we take your privacy concerns very seriously.

43. The Google Book of World Records

You can use Google as a big factbook to find out everything about anything – including the world's extremes. I call it the *Google Book of World Records*. To collect records, just search for "the world's highest mountain is ..." and similar phrases. Here are some of the results, false or true!

The highest mountain in the world: Mount Everest. Also, depending on how you measure: McKinley, Mauna Key.

The smallest animal in the world: An amoeba.

The ugliest animal: An ignorant human. Also: a giant stick insect.

The richest country in the world: Norway. Also available: Luxembourg.

The largest book in the world: A book located in a religious building in Mandalay, Burma (near the Golden Duck Chinese restaurant).

The fastest human alive: Charles Paddock.

The biggest city in the world: Reno, also known as "Little Las Vegas."

The world's smartest human: Cecil Adams.

The world's strongest human: Kuririn Kawaii of Dragonball.

The most expensive car: An old Rolls Royce saloon convertible from way back in the day, worth 40 million dollars.

The cheapest mode of transportation: By water, but water-borne commerce is limited in speed. Also cheap: Mini-bus, city-bus, Metro, and train.

The richest man in the world: Robson Walton. Strong contender: Bill Gates.

The best comic artist: Marc Silvestri.

The richest woman in the world: Claire Zachanassian.

The poorest country in the world: Mozambique.

The most complicated formula: The formula for calculations of the acoustic field of a slanted transducer in the far-field zone.

The most boring book: Learning and Using Communication Theories: A Student Guide for Theories of Human Communications, by Stephen W. Littlejohn.

The most expensive painting: Vincent van Gogh's "Portrait of Dr. Gachet."

The sweetest candy: The sweet-potato candy.

The hottest dish in the world: Taiwain Ramen (Wakaranai).

The spiciest chili is: "Mouseshit" chili that comes from the mountain. It's small but deadly!

The most shocking painting: "Grandma's Bad Attitude," a chalk street painting in San Mateo. It depicts a surly elderly woman's face, wrinkled with age, her tongue stuck out in disgust.

The fastest car in the world: Honda's V6 supercar.

The fastest superhero: Marvel's "Nova."

The coolest superhero: Superman.

The funniest sitcom: Rick Mercer's "Made in Canada."

The world's deadliest weapon: A Marine and his rifle.

The longest movie: Erich von Stroheim's 1925 silent movie "Greed."

The most evil nation: Contamination.

The most poisonous snake: Olive Sea Snake (on land: the Inland Taipan).

The most poisonous animal: The Dart Poison Frogs from Central and South America.

The world's cutest animal: The Swarovski silver crystal sea horse.

The most aggressive dog: An Akita.

The laziest animal: The Sloth.

The world's largest desert: The Sahara in Africa.

The world's most dangerous city: Baghdad.

The world's best dad: Homer Simpson.

The world's best mom: Thangamani of Varkala in Kerala.

The tastiest dish: Squirrels.

The prettiest woman in the world: Tonya Harding.

The fastest guitar player in the world: Jimi Hendrix.

The most famous living person: Harry Potter.

The best James Bond actor: Pierce Brosnan.

The best James Bond movie: Goldfinger.

The worst James Bond movie: A View to a Kill.

The most expensive movie ever made: Steven Spielberg's "War of the Worlds." (Also: James Cameron's "Titanic.")

The hippest actor: Brad Pitt.

The man with the best "six-pack" abs: Kwon-Sang Woo.

The person with the highest IQ in the world: Marilyn Vos Savant (with an IQ of 228).

The world's tallest man: The one who kneels down to help a child.

The world's sweetest fruit: Mango, produced in the island province of Guimaras.

The world's worst director: Ed Wood.

The busiest city in the world: Tokyo, Japan.

The world's worst smell: Cat urine.

The biggest problem in the world: That people do not understand each other.

The most heroic dramaturgical feat ever attempted by an American Playwright: August Wilson's ten plays ("Gem of the Ocean," "Joe Turner's Come and Gone," "Ma Rainey's Black Bottom," "The Piano Lesson," "Seven Guitars," "Fences," "Two Trains Running," "Jitney," "King Hedley II" and "Radio Golf").

The biggest detonation in history: A nuclear test at the Bikini Atolls.

The hottest temperature ever measured on earth: 58 degrees Celsius/ 136 degrees Fahrenheit, in Libya 1922.

The best place to spend holidays: At home.

The world's saddest movie: Grave of the Fireflies.

The world's funniest movie: Holy Grail, Life of Brian, and Napoleon Dynamite.

The world's slowest website: www.mozdev.org

The world's tallest building: The Taipei 101 in Taipei, Taiwan (1,670 feet).

The world's funniest joke[1]:

> Two hunters are out in the woods when one of them collapses. He doesn't seem to be breathing and his eyes are glazed.
>
> The other guy whips out his phone and calls the emergency services. He gasps: "My friend is dead! What can I do?" The operator says: "Calm down, I can help. First, let's make sure he's dead."
>
> There is a silence, then a shot is heard. Back on the phone, the guy says: "OK, now what?"

The most successful movie: Independence Day.

The most popular dish in the world: Blintz (also called Blintze, Blin or Blini), a thin pancake.

The best wine in the world: The wine that you like the most – no matter its country or origin or price level.

The best tennis player in the world: Roger Federer.

The best soccer player in the world: David Beckham.

The best pool player in the world: Jackie "Minnesota Fats" Gleason.

The world's most renowned expert on Osama bin Laden: Rohan Gunaratna.

The loudest sound on earth: A space shuttle launch.

The most expensive jewelry on the market today: Platinum jewelry, platinum engagement pins and rpins.

The most colorful mineral in the world: Fluorite.

The biggest airplane in the world: The An-225 Mriya.

The longest fight in history: Helio Gracie vs Valdemar Santana (3 hours and 45 minutes non-stop).

The deadliest martial art: Ju Jitsu in its purest form.

The most beautiful children's book: Jan Karon's "Miss Fannie's Hat."

The worst cook in the world: Dad.

End Notes

1. Diane King, Scotsman.com, on the LaughLab experiment conducted by Dr. Richard Wiseman, University of Hertfordshire. (www.55fun.com/43)

44. Spelling Errors Galore

Almost every spelling error you can think of has indeed been made at one time or another. It's only that before Google came along, we never knew all the places the misspelling was made, and by whom. That's changed now; among the billions of pages indexed, every celebrity, title, phrase, and word exists in dozens of variants. To see for yourself, just enter a misspelled word and ignore Google's spelling suggestion for a moment (and if you want to limited your search to only a certain news source, use the "site" operator, e.g. *site:cnn.com*).

Here's a "best of spelling," courtesy of the Google search engine:

"The leader of the Sudan Peoples' Liberation Movement/Army ... yesterday received a personal message from **US President George Hush Jr**, according to the rebel movement."
– *Afrol News, November 2005*

"This autumn, **Britney Pears** will launch her first perfume to US ... composed of flowers and vanilla."
– *Toutenparfum.com News, August 2004*

"At the current time, The MGM Grand does not have any confirmed information regarding a April 6th performance starring **Paul McMartney**."
– *BeatleLinks Fab Forum, February 2002*

"The Iranians are under pressure and the North Koreans are in disarray so in totality, the **war on error** it's been a huge progress in the past 12 months."
– *CNN.com International Transcript, March 2004*

"The **weapons of mass distraction** were not there and that's when we asserted that those weapons where there."
– *CNN.com Transcript, Debate Over U.S. Bid For International Involvment In Iraq, September 2003*

"There is public opinion and there is is public opinion. I'll give you my opinion. **Michael Jacksin** is innocent."
– *A Freudian slip? Michael Jackson Forum, Santa Barbara, California, September 2004*

"... Steven Speilberg ... Steven Spielburg ... Steven Spielberger ..."
— *Discussion thread on an E.T. forum*

"Favorite NFL Team: **an Francisco 49ers**"
— *What's an Francisco? Sports Illustrated*

"'Look at this **Angelina Jolly**,' Bridget's mother says in one of the new columns, presenting her as a role model."
—*International Herald Tribune, August 2005*

"Microsoft is hoping to gain a foothold. Also, **Goggle's** been there too, hoping to gain a foothold in the lucrative search engine market."
— *CNN Live Today, Transcript, February 2005*

 "Margaret Mitchell was born in Atlanta, Georgia ... In 1922 **she marred** Berrien Upshaw"
— *TeenReads.com, Margaret Mitchell Biography, 2003*

"If you don't know who Bruce Campbell is, you must have been living under a rock! He's only the biggest **B-Move Actor** ever"
— *Judy's Books member reviews, August 2005*

"Who is the fynest **male movie stair** of 2003???"
— *BestAndWorst.com Ballot*

45. Google Groups, Time Machine

Google Groups[1] is the name of Google's internet discussion group search engine. Not only does it let you search recent postings from the so-called Usenet, it also contains a huge archive going back to May 11, 1981. And this is where the fun starts.

By using the Google Groups advanced search options, you can set a posting start and end date for every search query. This way you can go back in time to find the earliest mentions of a celebrity, an idea, a company, or anything else starting from the 1980s. (Like the first mention of pop singer Madonna, or a first discussion about New Coke.) Sometimes, the way people talked about this "new thing" back then is interesting in itself. Also, you can find out about popular misconceptions, or predictions which are extremely off-target in retrospect.

A while ago, Google presented a "best of" timeline showing off gems from the "golden age of Usenet." The timeline was created with the help of Jürgen Christoffel, Kent Landfield, Bruce Jones, Henry Spencer, and David Wiseman. Following are portions of this timeline and its postings as well as my own findings.

Working on Tron

> We are currently working ... on the Disney/Lisberger production of TRON. This film will be a combination of computer animation, hand animation, optical image processing ("the Bob Able look") and live action. Only about 10% is live action. While the plot of TRON may be hard for hackers to take (its about computers, and so computer hackers will get picky about the details of the fantasy plotline) it looks like it will be very striking visually.
> – *Craig W. Reynolds via JPM, fa.sf-lovers, Jun 10 1981*

Microsoft Not Downwards-Compatible

> Several announcements have indicated that DOS 2.0 is compatible with DOS 1.1 ... In at least one instance, this is not true! In DOS 1.1, function 1Bh returns a pointer to ...
> – *Cdi in net.micro.pc, April 9 1983*

First Mention of MTV

You want to see re-dubs and lip-synchs check out MTV –
if your ears can take it...
— *Teklabs in net.music, Mar 22 1982*

Star Wars: Return of the Jedi

"Revenge of the Jedi"... Episode 6 in the Star Wars saga,
has just finished filming, according to some friends I have
down in Arizona. ... The release date for us humans that
want to see it is still the summer of 1983. I guess it takes
that long to score all the music, do all the film-editing,
prepare all the promo material, and all that junk.
— *Azure in net.movies, June 9 1982*

The Hitchhiker's Guide to the Galaxy

... appears weekly on PBS. (Fri in Toronto) very strange
but enjoyable sci-fi.
— *utcsstat in net.movies, August 6 1982*

The C64 Computer

Any opinions on the new Commodore 64 computer. I've
seen it and it looks pretty neat. (i) it comes with 64K of
memory standard (ii) in highest graphics resolution it has
320 X 200 pixels.
— *Doug in net.micro, Aug 21 1982*

Madonna's Early Years

I have heard a song with some chipmunk-voiced woman
singing 'We're living in a Material World' ... Question: Who
sings this?
— *Bob Switzer in net.music, January 17 1985*

The New "Terminator" Movie

'The Terminator' is better than I thought it would be. The coming attractions made it look like a fairly standard action film emphasizing multiple deaths. Well, that element is certainly present, but there is more to the film than violent killings. Not an awful lot more, but more.
– *Reiher in net.movies, November 5 1984*

First Usenet Mention of the Y2K Bug

I have a friend that raised an interesting question that I immediately tried to prove wrong. He is a programmer and has this notion that when we reach the year 2000, computers will not accept the new date. Will the computers assume that it is 1900, or will it even cause a problem? I violently opposed this because it seemed so meaningless.
– *Spencer Bolles net.bugs, Jan 19 1985*

The New Coke

Okay.... I've endured a lot of abuse in my time, but this is the final straw! **** They are changing the Coca-Cola formula!!!!!!!!!! **** Is nothing sacred??!!! They might as well outlaw the Beatles, or change God's name, or reinstate prohibition.
– *Gordon Howel in net.misc, April 26 1985*

First Mention of Bruce Willis

You all out there have been talking about ABC and whether anyone actually watches it anymore. Well, there's a show on ABC called "Moonlighting" that is actually not half-bad. It stars Cybil Shephard (there aren't too many better looking women on television) and Bruce Willis (I know, who???).
– *Jeff Gershengorn in net.tv, September 7 1985*

Early Review of Back to the Future

Let me be the first to recommend Back to the Future.
There's life yet in the Steven Spielberg's little world, which
had started to get a little shopworn with Goonies. All the
familiar Spielberg elements are there: popular non-science,
whacky nuclear family, small-town America, heartwarming
twists of plot ... Yet three things save this one, in high style:
1) Robert Zemeckis' direction. I don't know how he does
it, but somehow, without any particular style you can point
your finger at, he has developed the lightest touch in
movies, and I now believe that this man can put
ANYTHING over on you, and make you love it. 2) The
performance of the lead actor, whose name I don't even
know. He now joins Tom (Risky Business) Cruise and ...
(The Sure Thing) ... as the most appealling young comic
actors in America.
— *Steve Upstill in net.movies, June 30 1985*

First Mention of IRC

I have recently got ahold of a program called irc (Internet
Relay Chat) Each machine runs its own server and the
servers are link in a tree fashion to a master server. I've
only messed with it a little, but it appears to be a good
program.
— *Todd Ferguson in comp.sources.d, February 10 1989*

AOL Disks?

has this happened to anyone else? I have received 4 of
those AOL disks over the last year or so, and I have never
once taken them up on their free offers.
— *Scott, via Bruce Fletcher, around 1994*

Seinfeld

For those interested, Jerry Seinfeld's show has been
renewed for the fall season. A good move by NBC,
IMHO. If you haven't seen the show, check it out.
— *Brian Boguhn, via Larry Setlow, around 1990*

The World Wide Web Is Announced By Its Inventor

The WWW project merges the techniques of information
retrieval and hypertext to make an easy but powerful global
information system. ... The project started with the
philosophy that much academic information should be
freely available to anyone. ... The web contains documents
in many formats. Those documents which are hypertext,
(real or virtual) contain links to other documents, or places
within documents. All documents, whether real, virtual or
indexes, look similar to the reader and are contained within
the same addressing scheme.
– *Tim Berners-Lee in alt.hypertext, August 6 1991*

Douglas Adams Discovers the Net

Yeah, having jut discovered the Internet, I'm anxious that
I'm going to be spedning far too much time on it!
– *Douglas Adams in alt.fan.douglas-adams, October 5 1993*

Amazon CEO Looking for Help

Well-capitalized start-up seeks extremely talented
C/C++/Unix developers to help pioneer commerce on
the Internet. You must have experience designing and
building large and complex (yet maintainable) systems, and
you should be able to do so in about one-third the time
that most competent people think possible.
– *Jeff Bezos in mi.jobs, August 22 1994*

Friends, the New TV Show

This show is about 6 young friends living in the city. Time
will tell how much they are individuals and how much they
are merely caricatures. TV Guide tends toward the latter
view and also suggests it is, like 'Ellen', somewhat of an
attempt to copy 'Seinfeld'. There may be some truth to that
statement (part of the opening credits sequence is similar in
style to 'These Friends of Mine') but Friends is not a clone
of either of those shows and I think TV Guide was overly
pessimistic. There is plenty of room for several shows in

this genre.
– John F. Carr in rec.arts.tv, September 26 1994

What's Yahoo?

I have heard mention of a search utility called 'yahoo' on
some of my lists. Can anyone tell me what this is and
where I can find it?
– Ktrent in bit.listserv.help-net, January 17 1995

EBay Founder Promotes New Site

...www.ebay.com/aw/ ... All items are offered by the
individual sellers, and anyone is free to bid on any item, or
to add items, free of charge.
– Pierre Omidyar, misc.forsale.non-computer, September 12 1995

Google Too Cluttered

Google replaces the simple vote-count with an opaque
percentage, adds an unhelpful bar-graph for each response,
etc etc etc. ... Also, Google's search-page is bogged down
with ridiculous amounts of history/ theory/
acknowledgements, making it load much slower, and
menus that aren't really relevant for me.
– Jorn in comp.infosystems.search, April 1 1998

46. Growing a Google Word

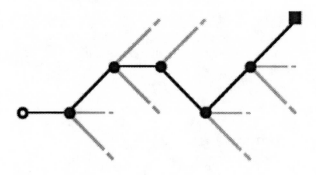

You can grow yourself a Google word, letter by letter, starting with any seed. Here are the rules to make it work.

Take any letter, or a couple of letters. Say, "bo." This is your seed word.

Now check the Google results for "bo**a**," "bo**b**," "bo**c**" and so on for all letters in the alphabet. Checking this letter by letter yourself is tedious, but you can automate this using FindForward (see findforward.com/?t=letter ... be patient when using this tool because it needs to check Google several times to return the results). Here's what we get:

boa = 654,000
bob = 13,400,000
boc = 876,000
bod = 536,000
boe = 303,000
bof = 213,000
bog = 8,390,000
boh = 126,000
boi = 269,000
boj = 133,000
bok = 649,000
bol = 601,000
bom = 652,000
bon = 2,760,000
boo = 832,000
bop = 503,000

boq = 21,600
bor = 604,000
bos = 800,000
bot = 1,600,000
bou = 141,000
bov = 186,000
bow = 2,030,000
box = 56,400,000
boy = 9,610,000
boz = 205,000
bo0 = 8,610
bo1 = 14,500
bo2 = 19,200
bo3 = 11,800
bo4 = 6,430
bo5 = 11,600
bo6 = 11,000
bo7 = 9,490
bo8 = 4,820
bo9 = 5,100

The one result with the highest page count in Google, you'll grow again – until you're either satisfied with the word, or you don't get any more results for it. The seed in our example, "bo," has the most result pages for "box." Of course... that's a common word. "Bob" is also quite popular because it's a name. (Other combinations, like "boz," are much less popular.) Now you continue with "box." The most popular continuation here is "boxe," probably because it means "box" in French. "Boxe" continues to grow into "Boxer," and I'm satisfied with this result so I won't grow it again. The seed word, bo, has grown into a boxer.

Similarly, "g" turns into "good," "h" into "have," and "my" into "myself." The letter "a" turns into the more cryptic "attori."

You can also grow numbers. For example, a 1 grows into a 100000. 1900 grows into 190000. 55 to 5500. If you use 194 as seed number, you can grow it to 1945 – the year World War II ended.

47. Most Popular Words, and PopSents

Which words are the most popular? Which words are most used online? We can find out by searching Google for every word in a dictionary – and then comparing the resulting page count for every word. Doing this, here are the 50 most popular English words. Before you take a look, can you guess which words will be on top?

(Of course, the data is slightly skewed, because the approach does not take into account how often a word appears on an individual page. This can give a slight boost to words which appear often on pages, but also mostly only once, like "copyright" or "home".)

1. the

2. of

3. and

4. to

5. a

6. in

7. for

8. on

9. home

10. is

11. by

12. all

13. this

14. with

15. about

16. or

17. at

18. from

19. are

20. us

21. site

22. information

23. you

24. contact

25. an

26. more

27. new

28. search

29. that

30. your

31. it

32. be

33. as

34. page

35. other

36. have

37. web

38. copyright

39. not

40. can

41. our

42. use

43. news

44. will

45. privacy

46. help

47. one

48. rights

49. we

50. if

And here are the *least popular* words from the dictionary used:

> Bowdlerise, baccarra, legitimatise, clothesbasket, pauperise, muckheap, disembroil, gaolbird, hedgehop, chimneybreast, underquote, lughole, overcapitalize, acknowedgement, telephotograph, rumourmonger, undernourish, shopsoiled, chopfallen, clarts, halfpennyworth, forrader, outmarch, ropedancer, stomachful, reafforest, mercerize, cardpunch, maulstick, fingerstall, outridden, latinise, popadum, dustsheet, winceyette, straphanging, jewelelry, palankeen, skidlid, nasalise, heelball, coalscuttle, iodise, hipbath, counterattraction, chatey, remilitarise, chifonnier, disendow, cowheel, overcapitalise, roodscreen, salify, slenderise, macadamise, scrumcap, borshcht, velarize, transistorise, checkrail, longhop, chapelgoer, lanternslide.

So there we have the most and least popular words. But what about full sentences? We can't find them automatically, unless we search for all word combinations – which would take forever. And because it's impossible to automate, people created a game for this: PopSents.

PopSent is short for "popular sentences." The goal of the game, which was invented by Larry Tapper, is to create a real and meaningful sentence which returns the most results in Google (compared to other sentences of the same word length).

For example, the sentence *"I am hungry"* (entered in quotes) returns 311,000 results. Not a lot when you consider how many pages Google has. So let's try something which might yield some more results: "I was born," which returns almost 8 million result pages – much better already.

The PopSents homepage (somethinkodd.com/popsents/) lists some of the most popular sentences found in a high-score table. Can you beat those?

3 Word Sentences

- "What's new"

- "You don't"

- "I don't"

- "You will be"

- "It is not"

4 Word Sentences

- "I don't know"

- "Click here for more"

- "This page uses frames"

- "Click here to see"

- "Do you want to"

5 Word Sentences

- "You don't have to"

- "Click here for more information"

- "I don't want to"

- "Tell us what you think"

6 Word Sentences

- "Your browser doesn't support them"

- "Email this page to a friend"

7 Word Sentences

- "tell me when this page updated"

- "an error occurred while processing this directive"

- "your use of this website constitutes acceptance"

8 Word Sentences

- "Trademarks are the property of their respective owners"

- "This site is best viewed with Internet Explorer"

48. Create Google Poetry, Prose, and Collages

Wanting connections, we found connections – always, everywhere, and between everything. The world exploded in a whirling network of kinships, where everything pointed to everything else, everything explained everything else ...
– Umberto Eco, Foucault's Pendulum (1988)

Can you write a text, like an essay, using only phrases which have at least a single result in Google (using quotes in your search)? Or to put it differently, can you write something using only words that have been written before – *using only thoughts of others?* Google prose and poetry is challenging and fun.

Of course, you need the Google search engine for this. For everything you want to express, search the first few words and take the completed sentence. Or think up a simple sentence which you suspect has been uttered somewhere, and verify this by checking if Google returns results.

On the following pages, you'll find my try at that. Afterwards, you can find out about Google rhymes, and Google collages.

A Strange Google Journey

(This is a free speech.
All sentences are quoted...
By using Google's search engine.
Everything I've found using Google.
Every single sentence I write from now on.
Just copy the line and paste it in your browser.
In occasional spots I've adjusted punctuation and paragraph breaks for greater clarity.
Every line belongs to one person.
Every line belongs to one organization.
Remember these are all true quotes.
Including the headline of the article.
Including this first paragraph.
I know you can google it yourself. Sometimes we lack in content, but we compensate with style.)

So, what is the meaning of life, really?
And are blogs going to 'usurp' big media?
(Big Media – as in 'Big Media, the homogenous monolith'.)
You realize, of course, that this may be the most dangerous part of our journey. Or any journey you've ever taken.
And so the Google journey began.

I wanted to write a text that is relevant so as to show students how physics applies in their everyday world.
I mean, everyday I go and I do things because I have to.
We all are forced to suppress our natural response to stress.
These days everybody wants a winner and athlete's are forced to or willing to do whatever it takes to win.

Mind you, the winner would have to fight Brian my killer radish.
OK, before this turns into another soap opera, we have seen email that a security site is down, and that is enough.
To Explain How to Answer a Call from Space.
Or rather, to explain the many elements that go into arranging and performing good tango music.
Seriously, this is all so awesome - thank you so much for finally making it easy for us to do something we've wanted to do for so long.

This text is actually a combination of computer-driven exercises.
This text is actually a blank Flash movie that has the text from the H1 tag pumped into it.
All it takes is Google to find them.
Of course, using random sentences wouldn't make a very good Italian sonnet.
Then again, Italians have long joked about being a nation of "saints and explorers," and space is, after all, the final frontier.

So, what is the "final frontier" in emulation technology?
Or technology in general as a means of saving education.
What is the final frontier? Ask any scientist and the likely answer will be "the ocean."
So, how does this work? Let us start with basic facts.
The function set made available to the genetic programming search for each sentence needing repair is derived from the set of partial analyses extracted.

I wanted to write a poem... but I didn't.
'Opus' means a 'work or construction'.
I guess I wanted to write about what we all want and can never have – the ability to rise above our lives.
After all, life has something serious in it.
Though not the kind of seriousness that sits heavily on the soul like puritan theology.
Not the kind of seriousness that seems to come along with a Billy Graham sermon, "This is your only chance!"

I just type the exact name of what I'm looking for, and start the search. Old Google hasn't let me down yet, I've found some real off the wall things.
I'm using google to post messages.
I'm using Google to think of stuff.
This is not everyday stuff here.
I mean, it's more complicated than that, but my point is...
I mean it's more like team work.

Success on the Web is a team effort.
A team effort that took the Brazilian men to victory.
What can be accomplished with a team effort that cannot be accomplished with individuals working separately.
Teams are unique, no two work exactly alike.
Teams are unique because they are comprised of young adolescents utilizing community technology centers as laboratories for their work.

The Web revolution is not about computers or technology.
What is the World Wide Web, really? What they know about you.
But who are they, exactly? What is their training, and what help can they offer you?
What is the web supposed to be? A resource for good quality content.
What is it the search engines are supposed to favor?
I believe search engines are still the ultimate form of advertising in terms of both the time and financial investment required.

Advertising today means working with electric e-commerce and traditional creativity, exploring the best possibilities.
Truth is or at least should be a basic principle in advertising as in all communication.
And this is just as important – if not more so – in online advertising as in any other marketing tactic.
That's because tactics are but means of achieving strategic objectives.
So, always plan strategy first.

Can you do a Full Corporate Murder Mystery for us?
Can you climb the Latin Mountain 1,000,000 M high?
How well can you use the web?
How well can you follow directions?
How well can you Spell?
How well can you write?

Questions. Nothing but questions, and unfortunately for the Indiana women's water polo team, there are still no answers.
Sounds crazy? Well, yes. Yes, it does.

It's crazy, because these will just write themselves since I've spent so much time thinking about them.

Language, metaphor, sentences out of nowhere, as if this miracle is something more – religious, blinding.

A rectangular matrix is populated with these words in random positions and directions.

Not Matrix the movie. I wish I hadnt given them my money.

The Matrix – that is, the world.

Our World, Your World, Europe in the Service of Globalisation with a Human Face.

This is not the "old Europe," as Rumsfeld says.

Come on, Rumsfeld is right – freedom is untidy!

(Everything I know I plagiarized in high school.)

Google is just so smart. Conversions, phone number lookups.

Real live conversations that surround me all day.

Every sentence you read or book that you flip through will affect your writing, just as every place you go and lesson you learn adds to the whole of your person.

Not only Google but also specialist search engines – plus the ones in between like Teoma.

I'm using quotes here a bit cynically.

Now I've written myself into a corner. At the heart of these "revelations" is truth. Yes, I'm using quotes.

Google this, Google that, Google Google Google.

(Google this, Google that. Is it always the best search engine? No.

For past two months, all we have heard is Google and nothing else in Silicon Valley.

Search engines are not the only means whereby people find sites.)

How else do you think the Dolphins escaped the Vogons?

Humanity needs to understand the Universe to survive. How many of us actually realize the importance of the present moment in the human history?

Humanity needs to know!

Humanity needs to make fundamental changes in how they live in, relate to and understand the world.

Just like dolphins we are of like mind and yet very individual in what each of us brings to the pod.

As living beings, we are woven into the web of life, just as all other life forms are woven into that web.

We are pure energy and totally interconnected with other living beings.

The Web makes it possible to assemble and integrate all those components into the text itself.

Because it is time, the eyes open, the body stands up, the hand stretches out, the fire is lit, the smile contends with night's wrinkles.
We grab what we think (what we hope) will fill our yearnings.
And in our hands, we will leave something as a legacy for society.

Evolution wants us to believe that species progress an infinite ladder upward.
We only act because the evolution wants us to spread our genes.
How can the dream of absolute liberty and the reality of absolute interdependence be resolved while our genes survive?
Will we survive if we lose two games, three games, maybe even five?

Especially in the last decade, liquidity, simultanaety, transparancy, and access for all bring to the ring not only the fittest of the fleet thinkers
In fact, the best of us are generalists who know a little about many things.
It's all about knowledge and learning. It's what I relish. It's how I live my life.
Divine life wants to learn first and then enjoy.
Life wants to help you to develop to your fullest potential, scoping out your options as you decide where you can contribute.

So next time you think of the cashier at the bank as other, when you see your parents or spouse as other, remember what you're doing to yourself.
If we are all striving to develop ourselves spiritually, then we should have something constructive to discuss.
Society these days has lost the lack of "communication" in the community, so we rely on the government to help us out instead of each other.
But society cannot transform the individual; it is the individual who can transform society. By negating the individual, it negated its own success.

With these things in mind, you should be just about ready to embark on your very own web logging journey.
If not in a blog, then in one of many possible ways.
May you always remember: those lives you have touched and who have touched yours are always a part of you.

Google Rhyming

An advanced variant of this game is to write poetry in rhymes. To write a Google rhyme, start off with any sentence. Like "I'm writing a book on love." Now you need to find the next line in Google, but it must rhyme on love. So you take a rhyme dictionary (www.rhymezone.com) and check what rhymes on "love." You'll find the words "dove," "glove," "shove," "above" and more. Now you replace all words in the original line except for "love" with the wildcard character asterisk "*" and search Google using quotes. In our case:

> The first line is: *"I'm writing a book on love"*
> So we search for: *"* * * * * above"*

This returns, among other lines, "room rates for the Inn Above." So with some creative words in-between we get:

> I'm writing a book on love
> And room rates for the inn above

... and we continue this approach until the poem is finished.

Creating Google Book Search Collages

Yet another way to recreate the words of others to produce something new is to use Google Book Search (books.google.com). Just think of a part of a sentence and then find it in a Google Book Search. Copy the highlighted text and its immediate surroundings into a paint program. The result is now made up of a variety of different books, and looks like this:

Now you can calmly decide whether to spend more time with

primary mark of linguistic competence is the capacity to create *new* sentences and to understand sentences one has never heard before.

the number of results displayed on each page to as many as 100, using the Google Search Preferences page, which is described in Chapter 7.

divination by means of air; and the fifth is divination by fire, which is called

Address Book search fields allow you to quickly find individuals in the address book.

regarding childbirth practices. This edict is detailed and extensive; it covers every imaginable activity that occurs in a maternity care unit, from

this type of book provides perspectives and insights that cannot be found in

Don't read every word – read only the highlighted texts to get the meaning.

49. Funny Google Videos

Google Video (video.google.com) is Google's video service where you can upload your own videos, or watch videos uploaded by others. You'll find anything from homemade college humor videos to short clips of *Family Guy*.

(If you can't watch the videos in your country, you can download the "FLV" files at the Google Video Downloader [www.55fun.com/49.2] site. The Google Video Downloader site also lets you see what others found worthwhile downloading, so it's a good place to find funny or interesting video.)

Here are some searches which might result in fun videos at Google Video.

Overworked Guy

Search for: *overworked*

You might find: A funny Asian clip of a couple in a restaurant. She complains he is spending too much time in front of the computer. I won't spoil what he does next...

Drunk Adults

Search for: *drunk*

You might find: Drunken people. (Which incidentally often makes for funny people.)

Highschool Dance

Search for: *"high school" dance*

Or search for: *"high school" music*

You might find: Incredible break-dancing. Or: an amateur dance group performing their Led Zeppelin choreography.

The Blue Man Group

Search for: *blue man*

You might find: The blue-skinned performance group which became famous in the Intel commercials.

Random Pranks

Search for: *prank*

You might find: All sorts of pranks, like a kid doing a prank phone call.

Costumes

Search for: *costume*

You might find: People dressed up in funny costumes – such as a Halloween dinosaur.

Humor

Search for: *satire*

Or search for: *humor... funny... parody... sketch... fun...*

You might find: People trying to play a sketch, play a prank, surprise someone or similar things.

Comedian

Search for: *comedian*

Or search for: *comedian... stand-up... joking... joke... seinfeld... conan...*

You might find: People telling jokes, like stand-up comedians or talk show hosts (e.g. Mitch Hedberg on the David Letterman Show).

Cartoons

Search for: *family guy*

Or search for: *simpsons...*

You might find: Short funny clips from the TV shows... like the Kool Aid Man making a surprise entrance.

Martial Arts

Search for: *karate*

Or search for: *jiu jitsu... tae kwon do... judo... boxing... martial arts*

You might find: Amateur recordings of martial arts performances or trainings. There's also an incredible *Karate chimp* waiting for you.

Napoleon Dynamite

Search for: *napoleon dynamite*

You might find: People dancing the dance from the end of the movie "Napoleon Dynamite" (some while wearing "Vote for Pedro" shirts). You can also see the "real" Napoleon Dynamite, Jon Heder, promoting the Utah State Fair. And then there's "Jamison Dynamite: The Return of the Star Wars Geek." (A similar dance to the one Napoleon performed can be found searching for *"Spiderman dancing,"* by the way.)

Amateur Singing

Search for: *karaoke*

You might find: Badly sung songs.

The Numa Numa Song

Search for: *numa numa*

You might find: Parodies of the parody of the "Numa numa" song by O-Zone.

Best of Cats

Search for: *funny cats*

You might find: A "best of" collection of funny cat clips that made its way around the internet.

The Star Wars Kid

Search for: *star wars kid*

You might find: A now famous amateur movie of a Jedi solo battle performed by an overachieving teen. (This was one of the many "memes" which took off at Andy Baio's Waxy.org.)

American Idols

Search for: *american idol*

You might find: Amateur singers, once again – including two-week wonder William Hung who said, "I want to make music my living."

Enter the Matrix

Search for: *matrix ping pong*

You might find: Two table tennis players in an amazing Matrix-like match.

Jerry Springer Talk Shows

Search for: *jerry springer*

You might find: "Darling, I'm a man, and not a woman" – clips taken from the infamous talk show which often happens to be more about fighting than talking.

Strange Weather Forecasts

Search for: *weatherman*

Also search for: *weather man*

You might find: Public broadcasts of rapping and dancing weather men. Or a weather man who suddenly starts swearing at Fox.

50. The Realplayer Fish, or: Telling a Story in Synonyms

Google has a nice synonyms feature built right into the main search engine. Using the "~" (tilde) operator preceding a word, you can search not only for the word itself but similar words as well. These aren't always synonyms (in the sense that they are different words with the same meaning); they are often simply *related* words with a different meaning.

To find out all the synonyms Google stores for a word, you can enter the word using the synonyms operator, but then exclude the word afterwards using the minus operator. Like here for the word "home":

~home -home

Since Google now can't show you results with "home," it must show you synonyms of home only. Those will be rendered in bold. If you want to find all the synonyms for a given term, you can continue excluding the synonyms you find until you hit an end and no more results are returned, like this:

~home -home -official -house -interior -homer -real-estate

That's already interesting, but you can also abuse Google synonyms. How? Just replace every word in a given story with Google's first synonym for that word! Of course, that's a boring task to do manually so I automated it. You can use the Synonym Storyteller tool (www.55fun.com/synonym/) to copy and paste your story. Hit submit, and it will be rendered in its synonyms for often surprising (and often, just nonsense) results.

As an example, here is the beginning of a fairy tale by the Brother's Grimm. It's called *The Fisherman and His Wife* and I will present a part of it first in its original wording, and afterwards, in a version which has been changed by the Synonym Storyteller (for the full tale, see authorama.com/grimms-fairy-tales-10.html).

The Fisherman and His Wife: The Original

There was once a fisherman who lived with his wife in a pigsty, close by the seaside. The fisherman used to go out all day long a-fishing; and one day, as he sat on the shore with his rod, looking at the sparkling waves and watching his line, all on a sudden his float was dragged away deep into the water: and in drawing it up he pulled out a great fish. But the fish said, "Pray let me live! I am not a real fish; I am an enchanted prince: put me in the water again, and let me go!" "Oh, ho!" said the man, "you need not make so many words about the matter; I will have nothing to do with a fish that can talk: so swim away, sir, as soon as you please!" Then he put him back into the water, and the fish darted straight down to the bottom, and left a long streak of blood behind him on the wave.

When the fisherman went home to his wife in the pigsty, he told her how he had caught a great fish, and how it had told him it was an enchanted prince, and how, on hearing it speak, he had let it go again. "Did not you ask it for anything?" said the wife, "we live very wretchedly here, in this nasty dirty pigsty; do go back and tell the fish we want a snug little cottage."

The fisherman did not much like the business: however, he went to the seashore; and when he came back there the water looked all yellow and green. And he stood at the water's edge, and said:

> "O man of the sea!
> Hearken to me!
> My wife Ilsabill
> Will have her own will,
> And hath sent me to beg a boon of thee!"

The Fisherman and His Wife: The Synonym Version

There was once a fisherman who lived with his daughter in a pigsty, closing by the seaside. The fisherman for sale to british out all holiday longest a-fishing; and 1 holiday, as he sat on the shor with his rodd, looking at the sparkling waves and watching his liner, all on a sudden his floating was dragged a way deep in to the water: and in cartoon it ups he pulled out a greater fish. But the fish said, "Pray letting millennium live! I am not a realplayer fish; I am an enchanted prince: putting millennium in the river again, and letting millennium go!" "Oh, ho!" said the manual, "you needing not build southern many dictionary about the matter; I will having nothingness to does with a fish that canned talk: southern pool a way, immigration, as soon as you please!" Then he putting him back in to the river, and the fish darted straight down to the bottom, and leftist a longest streak of blood behind him on the surf.

When the fisherman went official to his daughter in the pigsty, he told her how he had caught a greater fish, and how it had told him it was an enchanted prince, and how, on listening it learn, he had letting it british again. "Did not you asking it for anything?" said the daughter, "we radio cool wretchedly hear, in this nasty funny pigsty; does british back and telling the fish we want a snug tiny cottage.'

The fisherman mpd not muchmusic like the business: however, he went to the seashore; and when he come back there the river looked all business and environment. And he stood at the water's little thrill, and said:

"O manual of the sea!
Hearken to me!
My daughter Ilsabill
Will having her build will,
And hath sent millennium to beg a boon of thee!'

51. Google Parodies

Not all sites that *look* like Google *are* Google. Though there are some official humor-powered Google sites (like Google Klingon, Elmer Fudd Google, or "Google Pigeon Rank"), the following screens are all unofficial:

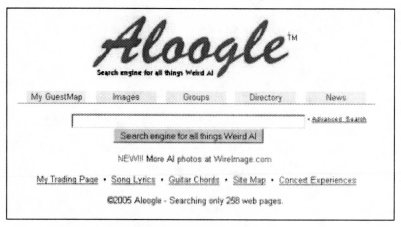

Aloogle searches all things Weird Al Yankovic.

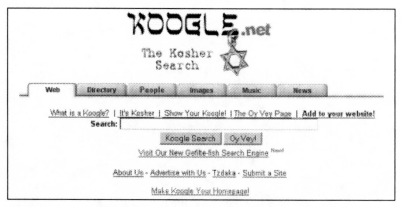

Koogle is "the kosher search"… a "Jewish" search engine.

Elgoog is Google... backwards (today, with a turkey for Thanksgiving).

Fo' shizzle my nizzle... Gizoogle is a gangsta-rap flavored Google.

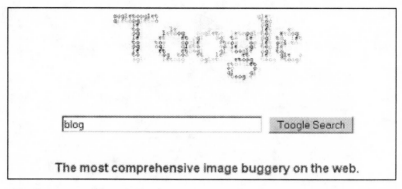

Toogle is a mix between Google parody and ASCII-art creator... enter any search term and a related image will show drawn with letters only.

Booble is censored here. This search engine had the honor of getting contacted by Google's Senior Trademark Lawyer, and was later on renamed to "Bible."

Spam Google finds nothing but spam. It's just like Google, without good results.

The Google FBI & CIA search. (By Semmelbroesel.)

Google April Fool's search was released on April 1st, 2004 as seemingly official Google search – it searches only pages related to April Fool's.

Cthuugle, the complete HP Lovecraft Search Engine.

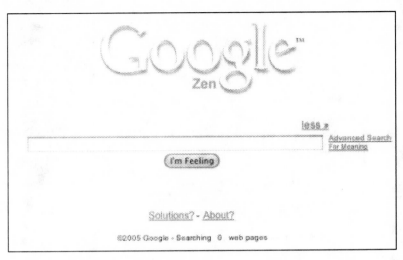

You can search 0 web pages with Google Zen. You might prefer hitting the "I'm feeling" button... (By X/Brooklyn.)

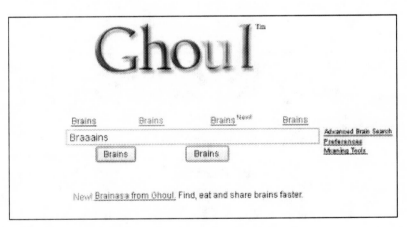

"Ghoul" searches for brains only...

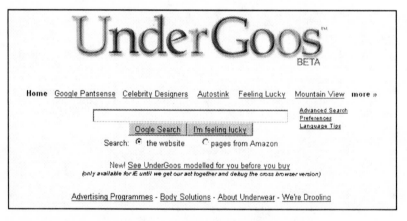

GOOGLE

Web   Images   Groups   News   Froogle

Please print query clearly: _____

Mail to: Google Search Request
1600 Amphitheatre Parkway
Mountain View, CA 94043

Please allow four to six weeks for results.

Google circa 1960. "Please print query clearly... mail to Google Search Request... and allow four to six weeks for results" (By Google employee Kevin Fox.)

UnderGoos
BETA

Home   Google Pantsense   Celebrity Designers   Autostink   Feeling Lucky   Mountain View   more »

Advanced Search
Preferences
Language Tips

Oogle Search   I'm feeling lucky

Search: ⦿ the website   ◯ pages from Amazon

New! See UnderGoos modelled for you before you buy
(only available for IE until we get our act together and debug the cross browser version)

Advertising Programmes - Body Solutions - About Underwear - We're Drooling

UnderGoos is a search engine for underwear.

Note: You can find the search engines shown here by searching for their title in Google – Aloogle, Koogle and so on (this is their "Googlonym," or "Memomark"… a bookmark that is a Google search). Sometimes, only a mock-up exists, and not a full-fledged search engine.

52. The Google Images Prediction Trick

This is a fun magic trick to fool your friends, colleagues or family. Here's how it *appears* to everyone around you:

- You open up Google Images and demand, "John, think of something."

- Your friend John says "I think of a yellow house."

- You type "What is it that John thinks of?" into Google Images, hit return, and boom – there are yellow houses in the results!

How It Really Works

Of course, neither Google nor you can predict the future or read your friend's mind (I assume!). So what's really happening? Just how can Google display *yellow houses*?

Because you told it to! The trick is incredibly simple: start by going to the fake Google homepage (www.55fun.com/52). Now though it appears as if you are typing "What is it ...," you actually type a slash "/" first. This starts hiding what you really type and replaces it with "What is it ...". So now, you type *yellow house* or whatever it is your friend mentioned. Finally, hit the slash key again and you can continue to type normally to enter the name of your friend or something similar.

Before you perform this trick in front of friends, make sure you practice it a little. If you do, your friends will not suspect a thing.

Note that if your friends are very tech-savvy or easy to get suspicious, you should replace the browser address – which reveals it's not the real Google – with the actual Google Images URL (without hitting return in the address bar, of course, because you don't want to leave the trick page).

53. Fun With Google Translations

There are many useful things to do with the Google Translator (you'll find it by clicking on "Language tools" next to the Google search box), but I won't discuss any of those here. Instead, I'll show you how to have fun creating nonsense texts by translating something back and forth!

Here's what to do. Pick any English text you like. Now paste it into the Google translator. Choose to translate it from English to French. Now copy the French translation into the box, and translate it back to English. Repeat for another round, and check what you've got.

The following example is the first paragraph from the White House George W. Bush biography:

> George W. Bush is the 43rd President of the United States. He was sworn into office on January 20, 2001, re-elected on November 2, 2004, and sworn in for a second term on January 20, 2005. Prior to his Presidency, President Bush served for 6 years as the 46th Governor of the State of Texas, where he earned a reputation for bipartisanship and as a compassionate conservative who shaped public policy based on the principles of limited government, personal responsibility, strong families, and local control.

What happens after translating it to French and back for two rounds? This:

> George W Bush is the forty-third chair of the United States. One swore to him in the office January 20, 2001, was re-elected November 2, 2004, and interior sworn in for a second limit January 20, 2005. Before his presidency, President Bush was useful during 6 years like the forty-sixth governor of the state of Texas, where it gained a reputation for the bipartisanship and like the conservative to sympathize who formed the law and the order based according to principles' of the limited government, the personal liability, of the strong families, and of the local order.

54. The Giant Google Painting

I'm not sure exactly what inspired artists Sembo and Yae of the artist group Exonemo (www.exonemo.com) to create a giant "landscape" painting of the Google homepage, but the results are interesting. The project started in December 2003, and was exhibited from February to April 2004 in Tokyo's *Mori Art Museum*. In Exonemo's words, the painting is "an analogization of a digital object." The digital is converted to the analog, but the analog is also converted back to the digital – because in his installation, Exonemo directed a webcam onto the painting and streamed the painting (and visitors around it) back online.

The following images are courtesy of Exonemo and document both the creation and exhibition of the project:

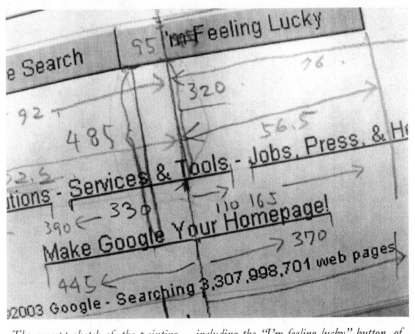

The concept sketch of the painting….including the "I'm feeling lucky" button, of course.

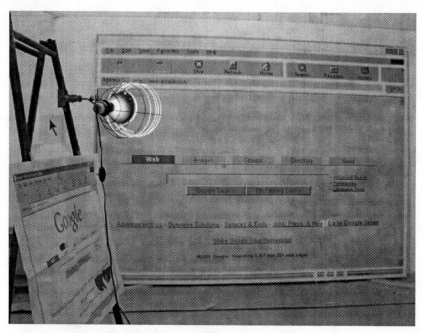

The painting is being created. A lamp illuminates the scene, and we can see the Google logo is still missing.

The painting is up.

Two visitors look at a projection from the camera.

A webcam snapshot from the exhibition.

Did anybody buy the painting? Yes, indeed — and no other than Google Inc themselves! Above you can see the painting being carried into the Google Japan office.

55. Googledromes

What's a Googledrome? It's a search on Google.com which yields the same top result no matter if it's spelled forward or backward. A Google palindrome, if you will, but the search itself may not be a perfect palindrome or consist of palindromes (the query must not stay the same in reverse, e.g. "rats live on no evil star" doesn't count, and also no two words in the query may be the reverse of each other, e.g. "palindrome emordnilap palindrome" doesn't count).

Further rules are that the search may contain only letters and numbers, and that there must be at least two letters in it (and at least two letters for every word in the query as well). Also, the result page may not in any way be prepared to be a target of this challenge.

Dave Pettit discovered the first Googledrome ever on March 15, 2006: it was *Oprah*... because a search for "oprah" and "harpo" (which is Oprah in reverse) returns the same number 1 result, oprah.com.

Can you find a Googledrome?

Acknowledgments

Thanks to all Google Blogoscoped readers who keep the blog running full steam with their tips and pointers in the forum, or by email*. Thanks to Iolaire McFadden for supporting me a great deal with formatting this book. Mark Draughn for English lessons, valuable feedback on this book, and adding bits and pieces here and there. Thanks to family and friends for the support; Justin Pfister, Tony Ruscoe, and Judith Lenssen for helping out with the book; everyone who provided material for this book, answered my questions, or allowed me to republish bits and pieces, including Jamie Grant, Douwe Osinga and Exonemo. Gary Price, Danny Sullivan, John Battelle, Nathan Weinberg and Miel Van Opstal for being great searchblogging buddies. The people who keep Google running, because frankly this book wouldn't exist without them. Markus Renschler and David Vise for helping on publication approaches. The beta readers for beta-reading, and the wiki writers of chapter 14. And thanks to Shan for disturbing me while writing!

*The top forum members as of April 2006 were /pd, Caleb E, Sam Davyson, Ionut Alex. Chitu, TOMHTML, Corsin Camichel, Tony Ruscoe, Justin Pfister, dpneal, Travis Harris, Brian Mingus, Niraj Sanghvi, Splasho, Ludwik Trammer, OREO, Brinke Guthrie, Andrew Hitchcock, Haochi, Yannick Mückenhirn, Kimspitstop.dk, or, Wouter Schut, Faderale, Josue R., Ades, Elias KAI, Nathan Weinberg, Support Freedom!, justin flavin, alek, orli yakuel, Pierre S, Utills, Milly, pokemo, Ashman, CJ Millisock, Tadeusz Szewczyk, Search-Engines-Web.com, Nate, Miel, Artem, Mark Draughn, Anthony Pennington, Hanan Cohen, SCJM, Iolaire McFadden, KenWong, Seth Finkelstein, Sale, Kirby Witmer, Bratsche, BrianS, Dimitar Vesselinov, Zoolander, Jason Schramm, RC, Hashim, Luca, pacificdave, Roger Browne, Garett Rogers, Ramibotros, Brian Brian, Jon Henshaw, Personman, Piotr Zgodzinski, Phil Defer, Daniel Brandt, Nanaki, Joey J., Kevin Fox, Natey, Richard M, George R, Corni, Sunil, Rich Hodge, John K, Tiago Serafim, Digital Inspiration, Veky, david sanger, bernis, jtdgrz, Pau Tomàs, Alterego, Hatem, Cow, Suresh S, Martin Wang, ardief, GamingFox, Shaun Robinson, Michael Schaap, Manu, Adam B., and Michael Fagan. Thanks guys!

Glossary

API *Application Programming Interface* (and other meanings); a library for programmers to more easily achieve certain tasks.

Backlink A link pointing from someone else's web page back to the page in question (e.g. your page). Usually the more (relevant) backlinks a page receives, the higher it ranks in Google for certain search queries.

BackRub The name given to the precursor to Google.

Blog A blog or weblog is an online news journal usually written by a single person or a small group, covering any imaginable subject. New entries are posted on top, often with a way to comment on the entry. The blogosphere or blogspace on the other hand is the "universe" of all blogs. Splogs are "spam blogs" which copy content from elsewhere to make money with ads. Vlogs are video blogs, and podcasts are blog-like audio shows that can be downloaded to the iPod or other MP3 players.

Cookie On the web, a small data file a website saves on your computer through your browser. This file is used to memorize e.g. a log-in status, or to better understand your browsing behavior.

Data center A Google data center is a group of servers delivering specific search results to you.

Deep web The kind of websites that are usually hidden from free search engines (either because they are paid content, or because the search engines do not understand how to crawl these sources).

Egogoogling To search for one's own name in Google. (Also: *autogoogling, egosurfing.*)

Google Google means either Google Inc., the company, or Google the web search engine, or – as in "to google" – it's a verb meaning "to search."

Google Algos A short-hand for "Google's algorithms," meaning the technical specifics of how Google ranks its result pages (the details of which are only really known to those who work at Google).

Google cache Google makes a copy of every website and allows searchers to view these copies (unless the webmaster prevents this with the "robots.txt" file, or so-called meta-tags).

Googlebomb A link campaign trying to discredit a group, company or person. Repeated links with the same link text are used to connect a negative Google search to a certain web page.

Googlebot This software program crawls (or "spiders") the web for content. The content is indexed and later appears in Google search results.

Googlebowling A rumored black-hat methodology to hurt a competitor's website through a link campaign.

Googledance Noticeable updates to the structure of the Google result rankings. (Some major "Google updates" are even given names, like "Google Florida.")

Googlefight Putting two search queries against each other to see which one returns the highest page count on the Google results page.

Googlejuice The popularity that makes a web page appear high in Google search results. For example, "to give someone Googlejuice" can mean to link to someone (because a link to another page increases its value in the eyes of Google). A site which has "a lot of Googlejuice" is usually a web page with a high PageRank.

Googleplex The Mountain View headquarters of Google Inc.

Googler An employee of Google Inc. (a Noogler on the other hand is a new Google employee, and a Xoogler is an Ex-Google employee).

Googlewhack Finding only a single result using two words from the dictionary.

Googlosophy The science of all things Google.

Googol A 1 followed by 100 zeroes. The Google founders often quote this word as origin of how they came up with the word "Google."

IP Often a shorthand for *Internet Protocol address*, meaning the uniquely identifiable number your computer has when you're online.

Meme On the web, this refers to an idea that quickly spreads from one site to another, virus-like.

Meta search A search engine which itself uses other search engines to determine its results.

Onebox result For certain searches, Google displays an info-box above the actual organic search results. This box may display more direct information (like the answer to a question), or a link to related services (like Google News).

Operator A syntax command to trigger specific Google search functionality. For example, the *site* operator (as in "*site:searchenginewatch.com/blog*") allows you to restrict your search to a single domain.

Page count The Google page count is an approximate number telling the searcher on how many web pages the terms in the query appear. For example, searching for "the" returns over 18 billion pages at this time (Google only allows you to see the first 1,000 results for any single search, though).

PageRank The general "value" of a website in the eyes of Google. In a nut-shell, the value is derived from analysis of how many pages link to a certain page (and also, how many pages link to the pages that link to a certain page!). Usually, the higher the PageRank, the more likely this page appears on top of search results often. This value ranges from 0-10, with 10 being the best (and most rare) of values. New websites will always start out with a "PR" of 0. You can check a page's PageRank by installing the Google Toolbar for your browser.

Phrase search When you put quotes around your Google search query, Google only finds exact (or almost exact) matches.

RSS *Really Simple Syndication* (and other meanings), a feed format allowing you to subscribe to a blog or other regularly updated online content.

SEO Search Engine Optimization; the art (sometimes: *dark art*) of bringing websites on top of search engine results. An SEO contest is a competition to bring your own site on top of search engines – usually Google – for a specific search. There are black-hat and white-hat SEO strategies (the black-hat strategies can result in a website being "Googleaxed," also known as the Google Death Penalty, a full ban within the Google search results).

Stop words Traditionally, words like "the" or "a" which search engines ignore (Google doesn't have these stop words anymore).

Weblog → *See blog*

Printed in the United States
80693LV00004B/63